Athlone French Poets

PAUL VERLAINE
Sagesse

PAUL VERLAINE

Sagesse

edited by
C. CHADWICK

UNIVERSITY OF LONDON
THE ATHLONE PRESS
1973

Published by
THE ATHLONE PRESS
UNIVERSITY OF LONDON
at 4 Gower Street, London WC1

Distributed by
Tiptree Book Services Ltd
Tiptree, Essex

U.S.A. and Canada
Humanities Press Inc
New York

0 485 14704 1 *cloth*
0 485 12704 0 *paperback*

Printed in Great Britain by
The Garden City Press Limited
Letchworth, Hertfordshire
SG6 1JS

Athlone French Poets

General Editor EILEEN LE BRETON

This series is designed to provide students and general readers with both Monographs of important nineteenth- and twentieth-century French poets and Critical Editions of representative works by these poets.

The Monographs aim at presenting the essential biographical facts while placing the poet in his social and intellectual context. They contain a detailed analysis of his poetical works and, where appropriate, a brief account of his other writings. His literary reputation is examined and his contribution to the development of French poetry is assessed, as is also his impact on other literatures. A selection of critical views and a bibliography are appended.

The Critical Editions contain a substantial introduction aimed at presenting each work against its historical background as well as studying its genre, structure, themes, style, etc. and highlighting its relevance for today. The text given is the complete text of the original edition. It is followed by full commentaries on the poems and annotation of the text, including variant readings when these are of real significance, and a select bibliography.

E. Le B.

CONTENTS

INTRODUCTION

THE BIOGRAPHICAL BACKGROUND

The first edition of *Sagesse* bears the date 1881, but although some of the poems in the volume were written only a few months before it was printed towards the end of 1880, the earliest poem in it dates from the middle of 1872. *Sagesse* therefore covers a considerably longer period of time than Verlaine's previous volumes of verse, *Poèmes saturniens* published in 1866, *Fêtes galantes* published in 1869, *La Bonne Chanson* printed in 1870, though not actually published until 1872, and *Romances sans Paroles* published in 1874.

In the course of the eight years during which the poems of *Sagesse* were written Verlaine's life underwent several radical changes that are reflected in his poetry. The summer of 1873 in particular was undoubtedly one of the major turning points in his life. It was on 10 July that year, in Brussels, as the final episode in a violent quarrel that had flared up in London a few days earlier, that he shot and wounded his fellow poet, Arthur Rimbaud, who had been his close companion since the end of 1871. Verlaine was arrested and condemned to two years' imprisonment, the first weeks of which were spent in Brussels before he was transferred to Mons shortly after 27 August when the Court of Appeal confirmed the sentence passed at his trial on 8 August.

This breakdown of Verlaine's relationship with Rimbaud had a profound effect on him and there is good reason to think that he began to turn for consolation towards the Christian religion as soon as he entered prison. He had in any case never really succeeded in breaking free from his Christian upbringing, as the section of Rimbaud's *Une Saison en Enfer* subtitled 'Vierge folle— l'Epoux infernal' amply proves and as does Verlaine's sonnet in *Jadis et Naguère*, 'Vers pour être calomnié' with its anxious plea to the sleeping Rimbaud in the final line: 'Vite, éveille-toi. Dis, l'âme est immortelle?'. In prison the atmosphere was naturally conducive to turning the thoughts of the prisoners in a religious direction. Grace was said before and after meals, as Verlaine recalls twenty years later in *Mes Prisons* published in 1893, and

2 *Introduction*

mass on Sundays was obligatory with 'vêpres et salut, chantés par les détenus' (*Œuvres complètes*, ii, p. 767). His reading too may well have been guided along lines chosen by the prison authorities in view of his reference, in a letter to his friend Edmond Lepelletier dated 22 November 1873, to the fact that, among the English books he read to improve his knowledge of the language, was Cardinal Wiseman's religious novel *Fabiola*, while in a later letter, dated 27 March 1874, he refers to another Catholic novel, well-known at the time, *Ellen Middleton* by Lady Gullerton (*Correspondance*, i, pp. 112 and 135–6).

His writing began to follow the same direction as his reading and the poem 'Crimen Amoris' which Verlaine refers to as being already completed in a letter to Lepelletier dated 'Mons, du 24 au 28 novembre 1873' (*Correspondance*, i, p. 120) ends with the Satanic figure who dominates the early part of the poem and who clearly represents Rimbaud, being defeated by 'quelqu'un de fort et de juste assurément', while the final stanza of the poem is an appeal to 'le Dieu clément qui nous gardera du mal'. In the same letter to Lepelletier Verlaine writes: 'Je fais des "Cantiques à Marie" . . . et des prières de la primitive Eglise', and he includes an example of the latter which ends with the lines:

> Sauve notre cœur que le mal encient,
> Sauve-nous Seigneur, et confonds l'Impie!

In another letter to Lepelletier written at about the same time (*Correspondance*, i, p. 129), Verlaine enclosed a poem later to be entitled 'Sonnet boiteux' in *Jadis et Naguère* in which he refers to his 'affreux passé' with Rimbaud in London and calls down 'le feu du ciel sur cette ville de la Bible'.

There seems therefore little doubt that Verlaine's thoughts had already turned in a religious direction by the end of the year 1873, but it was not until the month of April in 1874 that the blow fell which finally led to his conversion or, to be strictly accurate, his re-conversion to the Catholic faith in which he had been brought up and from which he had tried unsuccessfully to break away under the influence of Rimbaud. During the first months of his imprisonment Verlaine had continued to hope for a reconciliation with his wife, despite the fact that she had begun legal proceedings against him as a result of his desertion of her some months before. But Mathilde Verlaine refused to consider any such reconciliation and on 24 April 1874 she was granted a separation from her husband and was given custody of their two-year-old child. On hearing this news 'je tombai en larmes sur mon pauvre dos sur mon pauvre lit' as Verlaine expressed it in *Mes Prisons* (*Œuvres complètes*, ii, p. 769). He asked the prison chaplain for a catechism, the *Catéchisme de persévérance* by Mgr. Gaume, in order to prepare himself for his formal return to the Catholic faith which may be said to have taken place when he took communion, for the first time for many years, on 15 August 1874, 'cet inoubliable jour de l'Assomption 1874' as Verlaine still remembered it almost twenty years later (*Œuvres complètes*, ii, p. 776), not perhaps without some intention of dramatising his conversion and making it appear a less gradual process than it in fact was.

As a result of his exemplary conduct in prison Verlaine was granted six months remission of his sentence which came to an end on 16 January 1875. Two months later he left for England, having spent a great deal of his time in prison 'piochant l'anglais à mort', as he put it in a letter to Lepelletier (*Correspondance*, i, p. 116), and having read not only the two novels mentioned above but the whole of Shakespeare in the original, according to a letter to Lepelletier dated 8 September 1874 (*Correspondance*, i, p. 147), and at least one short story by Dickens which he had in fact translated and had discussed with Lepelletier, in a letter dated 27 March 1874, the possibility of selling it to a magazine (*Correspondance*, i, p. 136).

Verlaine had already spent about six months in England with Rimbaud some two years before, enjoying the excitement of living in London, but this time his stay was to be of a very different nature since he took up a teaching post in the small town of Stickney about ten miles north of Boston in Lincolnshire. There he led a quiet and orderly life for the remainder of 1875 and the early part of 1876, extending his reading still further to include religious works such as St. Thomas Aquinas's *Summa Theologica*, St. Theresa of Avila's *The Way to Perfection* and Bunyan's *Pilgrim's Progress* according to letters to another of his correspondents, Ernest Delahaye, dated 3 September and 27 November 1875 (*Correspondance*, iii, pp. 109–12). These works are also mentioned, along with the poetry of Tennyson and Longfellow, in a letter to a third correspondent, Emile Blémont, dated 19 November 1875, while a further letter to Blémont, dated 8 February 1876, refers to works by Browning and Swinburne (*Correspondance*, ii, pp. 15 and 18).

Shortly after this date however, the peace and quiet of Stickney, which Verlaine had at first so much appreciated, began to pall and he moved to the neighbouring town of Boston in the spring of 1876 in the hope of making a living by giving private French lessons. But by 23 May he still had no more than three pupils, as he plaintively told Delahaye in a letter written on that date (*Correspondance*, iii, p. 115), and had decided to give up his attempt at setting up a private school and to leave for London in June with a view to finding another teaching post in the autumn. He found one in Bournemouth and stayed there from September 1876 until September 1877 when he returned to France to take up a teaching post at Rethel near Reims, before making a final brief stay in England when he taught at a school in Lymington, near Bournemouth, in the autumn of 1879. After this he not only left England for good but he also left the teaching profession and tried his hand instead at farming in northern France, with a notable lack of success.

By this time however Verlaine's period of 'sagesse' was over, in both senses of the term. That is to say that on the one hand his long years of good conduct were coming to an end (while at Rethel he had struck up a close friendship with one of his pupils, Lucien Létinois, who was to become, in some ways, almost a second Rimbaud in his life, and it was in fact with Létinois that he returned to England in 1879, obtaining for his *protégé* the post he himself had previously held at Stickney, and with Létinois too that he made his abortive attempt to set up as a farmer) and on the other hand the poems that reflected these years during which Verlaine had tried, as he put it, to 'réédifier sa vie' and were to make up the first edition of *Sagesse* had all been written.

THE COMPOSITION OF SAGESSE

Verlaine did not however have *Sagesse* in mind right from the beginning of the period which it covers. He at first intended to publish a volume consisting of thirty-two poems composed, for the most part, during his eighteen months' imprisonment and bearing the apt title of *Cellulairement*. These poems were of very different kinds, some, such as 'Crimen Amoris', being concerned with his past life with Rimbaud, others, such as 'Impression fausse', commenting on life in prison, at least one, the celebrated 'Art poétique', dealing with literary matters, and no more than two, 'Du fond du grabat' and 'Mon Dieu m'a dit' . . ., under the titles of 'Via dolorosa' and 'Final' respectively, being of an obviously religious nature. But Verlaine had no sooner finished copying out the manuscript of *Cellulairement* in October 1875 than he abandoned the idea of a volume whose unity would have been purely superficial, arising merely from the fact that all the poems in it had been written in prison, even though some may have been initially inspired shortly before July 1873 and many were no doubt substantially altered when Verlaine worked on them in the summer of 1875. He decided instead in favour of a volume with a deeper unity arising, if not always from the specifically religious nature of the poems it contained, at least from their grave moral tone. This meant that, of the thirty-two poems in the abandoned *Cellulairement* Verlaine held back twenty-five for use in later volumes he was to publish, particularly *Jadis et Naguère* and *Parallèlement*, and incorporated only seven into the new volume for which, after some hesitation, he had, by 1877, fixed on the title *Sagesse*.

Five of these, placed in the last of the three sections into which, with no regard for chronology, *Sagesse* is divided, were written in the summer of 1873, namely 'L'espoir luit . . .' (III iii), 'Gaspard Hauser chante' (III iv), 'Un grand sommeil noir . . .' (III v), 'Je ne sais pourquoi . . .) (III vii) and 'La bise se rue . . .' (III xi). These are in no way religious in tone, despite the sadness and distress they express as a result of the events of July and August 1873, nor are two other poems of the same kind, also inserted in the third section of *Sagesse*, which do not, for some reason, figure in *Cellulairement*, although one was composed shortly before and the other shortly after Verlaine's arrival in prison, 'Le son du cor s'afflige vers les bois . . .' (III ix) and 'Le ciel est, par-dessus le toit . . .' (III vi). To these must be added another poem written as early as 1872, 'Tournez, tournez, bons chevaux de bois . . .' (III xvii) which had also been included, in a slightly different form, in *Romances sans Paroles*, and no doubt to avoid this duplication, was dropped from the second edition of *Sagesse*. The sixth poem from *Cellulairement* to be included in *Sagesse*, again in the third section, was 'Du fond du grabat . . .' (III ii) dating from the summer of 1874, immediately before Verlaine's conversion, as the whole tone of the poem suggests. The seventh and final poem from *Cellulairement* was the sequence of ten sonnets in the form of a dialogue between Verlaine and God which, anachronistically in relation to the poems in the third section already mentioned, forms the climax of the second and specifically religious section of *Sagesse* and constitutes the heart of the volume as a whole. Though there is some slight confusion, as so often with the poems of *Sagesse*, about the date of this sonnet sequence beginning 'Mon Dieu m'a dit . . .' (II iv), there seems little doubt that it was written immediately after and as a result of Verlaine's communion on 15 August 1874. There seems equally little doubt that it was shortly afterwards that he wrote another poem charged with a strong religious feeling 'Parfums, couleurs, systèmes, lois . . .' (III viii) and although, like 'Le ciel est, par-dessus le toit . . .' and 'Le son du cor s'afflige vers les bois . . .', it did not figure in *Cellulairement*, it too found a place in *Sagesse*, not however in the second section but in the third.

These eleven poems, seven from *Cellulairement* and four others, are the only ones in *Sagesse* to have been composed in prison, or even, in the case of 'Tournez, tournez, bons chevaux de bois . . .', 'Le son du cor s'afflige vers les bois . . .' and perhaps 'Je ne sais pourquoi . . .', before Verlaine's imprisonment. This means that the vast majority of the poems in the latter volume, thirty-six out of the forty-seven in the first edition, are concerned not with the conversion and the events leading up to it in the years 1873 and 1874 but with the consequences of the conversion over a period of several years from 1875 to 1880.

THE THEMES OF SAGESSE

One of the most important of these consequences was the poet's firm determination to resist the temptations of the flesh, and a good many poems are concerned with this theme. Four of the most notable of them were written when he returned from Stickney to Arras on holiday in the summer of 1875 and were placed, with the usual disregard for chronology, early in the first section of *Sagesse*, 'J'avais peiné comme Sisyphe...' (I ii), 'Beauté des femmes...' (I v), 'Les faux beaux jours...' (I vii) and 'La vie humble...' (I viii). But he had already written one of the most powerful poems of this kind shortly before, while still at Stickney, 'Voix de l'Orgueil...' (I xix), and he was to continue to treat this theme sporadically over the next few years, inserting in the first section of *Sagesse*, irrespective of their date of composition, all the poems concerned, namely 'O vous comme un qui boite au loin...' (I vi), dating in all probability from 1876, and four pieces whose date is uncertain, 'L'ennemi se déguise en ennui...' (I xx), 'Va ton chemin...' (I xxi), 'Pourquoi triste, ô mon âme...' (I xxii) and 'Né l'enfant des grandes villes...' (I xxiii).

Associated with this theme of resistance to temptation is the theme of recognition of those forces which, however paradoxically on occasions, enabled Verlaine to succeed in his efforts. The first of these, written at Stickney in the summer of 1875, is 'Bon chevalier masqué...' (I i), anachronistically but none the less aptly placed as the opening poem of *Sagesse* since it expresses Verlaine's gratitude for his misfortune which has turned out to be the best of good fortune. A rather different kind of antithesis occurs in 'L'âme antique...' (I xxiv), in which Verlaine contrasts the classical and Christian concepts of grief, and in 'Qu'en dis-tu, voyageur...' (I iii), in which he contrasts the cynical, selfish attitude to life that he and Rimbaud once shared, with his present resolve to live a very different kind of life. 'Malheureux, tous les dons...' (I iv) might be said to reverse this antithesis in that Verlaine castigates Rimbaud, and by extension himself, for having flung away the benefits of a Christian upbringing, whilst 'La tristesse, la langueur du corps humain...' (III x) is a meditation on the frailty of human flesh inspired by Verlaine's past experiences.

But Verlaine did not limit himself to looking back on his past and drawing lessons from it; he also looked forward to the future in a poem which he wrote in celebration of the Virgin Mary, 'Je

ne veux plus aimer que ma mère Marie . . .' (II ii), which was
followed, shortly after he returned to Stickney, by a poem in
which he offered himself to God, 'O mon Dieu, vous m'avez
blessé d'amour . . .' (II i), a theme to which he returned much
later at Rethel in 1878 with the poem, 'Vous êtes calme, vous
voulez un voeu discret . . .' (II iii). These three poems from
different periods, along with the sonnet sequence, constitute the
whole of the short second section of *Sagesse*, but something of the
same tone of extreme piety permeates two poems added to
the second edition of *Sagesse* in 1889, 'Toutes les amours de la
terre . . .' and 'Sainte Thérèse veut que la pauvreté . . .' These
however were placed in the third section, no doubt because they
were substituted for the poem withdrawn from the same place,
'Tournez, tournez, bons chevaux de bois . . .' (III xvii).

Another category of poems which may be usefully distin-
guished in *Sagesse* is formed by those which are of a historical or
political nature. Among the best known of these are the two
sonnets written during the fruitful weeks at Arras in 1875,
'Sagesse d'un Louis Racine . . .' (I ix) and 'Non, il fut gallican ce
siècle . . .' (I x), in which Verlaine turned first to the seventeenth
century and then to the Middle Ages to find a kind of faith
similar to his own. He was however more interested in contem-
porary events and he launched a violent attack on the
Republicans, whom he considered as rationalists and atheists,
first in 'Petits amis qui sûtes nous prouver . . .' (I xi) and later in
the companion piece 'Or, vous voici promus, petits amis . . .' (I
xii). Though the date of these poems is uncertain, the first was
probably written in 1875 and the second may well have been
written as late as 1879 after one of the many electoral successes
the Republicans scored during these years. Another political
poem certainly composed in 1879 was added to them in the first
section 'Prince mort en soldat . . .' (I xiii) which commemorates
the death, on 1 June that year, of the Prince Imperial, the son of
Napoleon III, Verlaine's conversion to Catholicism having been
accompanied by a conversion to Royalism or, failing that, to
Imperialism, either of which he considered infinitely preferable
to Republicanism. Finally in 1880, in 'Vous reviendrez
bientôt . . .' (I xiv), Verlaine deplored the eviction of the Jesuits
from their house in the Rue de Sèvres on 30 June 1880, one of

the many harsh measures taken against them by the Third Republic.

A further group of poems in *Sagesse* is constituted by the four poems inspired by an attempt on Verlaine's part at a reconciliation with his wife and child, 'On n'offense que Dieu qui seul pardonne . . .' (I xv), 'Ecoutez la chanson bien douce . . .' (I xvi), 'Les chères mains . . .' (I xvii) and 'J'ai revu l'enfant unique . . .' (I xviii), all four of them probably written in 1878.

Much less clearly defined, although much larger, is the category of poems made up by the landscapes in which Verlaine took refuge from the temptations which he tended to associate with city life, despite the admiration for London he expressed in 'L'immensité de l'humanité . . .' (III xiv). This preference for the countryside is the theme of 'Désormais le Sage . . .' (III i), written as early as the summer of 1875 at Arras, though it had in fact already been preceded by one of the most celebrated of these peaceful scenes of *Sagesse*, written a short time before at Stickney, 'L'échelonnement des haies . . .' (III xiii). At roughly the same time as 'Désormais le Sage . . .' Verlaine wrote 'Vous voilà, vous voilà, pauvres bonnes pensées . . .' (III xii) which can be classed as a landscape in that Verlaine develops an analogy between his thoughts and a flock of sheep, but it was in the year 1877 especially that he seems to have found solace in nature with 'La mer est plus belle . . .' (III xv) written at Bournemouth and three poems written at Arras, 'La "grande ville" . . .' (III xvi), 'Parisien, mon frère . . .' (III xix) and 'C'est la fête du blé . . .' (III xx).

From this survey of *Sagesse* it can be seen that not only did Verlaine disregard chronology completely, but that he was by no means strict in arranging his poems according to their themes. It is true that all four poems in the short central section are of a decidedly religious nature while the much longer opening section is dominated by poems concerned with the defeat of temptation and the almost equally long final section by peaceful landscapes. The theme of victory over temptation however, although it begins and ends the first section, is interrupted by the two historical sonnets (ix and x), by the four poems with a political flavour (xi–xiv) and by the four poems inspired by Verlaine's attempt at a reconciliation with his wife (xv–xviii). Similarly in the third section, the last verse of the first poem, 'Désormais le sage...', seems like an introduction to the series of peaceful landscapes, but it is in fact followed by five poems of sadness and distress (iii–vii), flanked by two religious poems (ii and viii), and it is not until the ninth poem that the landscapes can be said to begin. Even then they are promptly interrupted by the sonnet on the frailty of the flesh (x) and, in the 1889 edition, by the two religious poems with which Verlaine replaced 'Tournez, tournez, bons chevaux de bois...' (xvii).

THE STYLE OF SAGESSE

In view of the fairly extensive period of time over which they were composed and in view of their widely different themes, it is not surprising that the poems of *Sagesse* should vary considerably in their style.

The earliest poems in the volume are, generally speaking, the most typically 'Verlainian'. They have, for the most part, the twilight atmosphere and the hesitant rhythm which constitute the distinctive features of so many poems in Verlaine's first volumes of verse and, like them, they tend, by these means, to suggest and to convey, rather than to describe and analyse the mood of uncertainty and the sense of instability which the poet had so often expressed in *Poèmes saturniens*, *Fêtes galantes* and *Romances sans Paroles* and which he continued to feel up to the time of his conversion.

'Le son du cor...' (III ix), for example, with its description of a sombre landscape behind which can be discerned Verlaine's own profound sadness, clearly belongs to the same category of poems as, for instance, 'Chanson d'automne' in *Poèmes saturniens* and 'Dans l'interminable Ennui de la plaine...' in *Romances sans Paroles*. 'Je ne sais pourquoi...' (III vii) is reminiscent of several of the *Ariettes oubliées* in the latter volume with the same anxious and questioning note and the same sombre and troubled atmosphere created by such expressions as 'esprit amer', 'aile inquiète et folle', 'aile d'effroi', 'essor mélancolique', 'tiède demi-sommeil', 'l'aile toute meurtrie' and 'tristement crie'. 'Un grand sommeil noir...' (III v) conjures up, in the final verse, a picture of a child seeking shelter in the depths of a cellar, and although the opening lines of the poem make the symbolic significance of this image fairly clear, this is not the case with 'L'espoir luit . . .' (III iii) where it is left largely to the reader to interpret the deeper meaning of the darkened room lit by a single ray of light. 'Du fond du grabat . . .' (III ii) has the same mysterious suggestive quality in the dark, winter landscapes of the opening verses and the shadowy figures of the later verses.

Not only are these poems thus typically 'Verlainian' in their tonality and in the mood which this conveys, but they are also very like much of Verlaine's earlier poetry in their absence of rhetoric and their impression of spontaneity and casualness. Even though 'L'espoir luit . . .' for example, has the highly formal structure of a sonnet in alexandrines, Verlaine succeeds in damping down any declamatory tone by using a simple vocabulary and an uncomplicated syntax and by making no attempt to avoid repeating, in an apparently careless way, the same, or similar words and phrases—'l'espoir luit comme un brin de paille dans l'étable' and 'l'espoir luit comme un caillou dans un creux', 'pauvre âme pâle' and 'pauvres malheureux', 'que ne t'endormais-tu', 'dors après', 'il dort' and 'va, dors'. This is also true of 'Le ciel est, par-dessus le toit . . .' (III vi), where the third line of each verse is almost, but not quite, a repetition of the first line of each verse and where the vocabulary and syntax are again extremely simple, as they are too in 'Un grand sommeil noir . . .' and 'Du fond du grabat . . .'

In these early poems of *Sagesse* Verlaine also shows the same preference as in *Romances sans Paroles* for short lines and 'vers impairs'. It is true that 'L'espoir luit . . .' is in alexandrines and 'Le son du cor . . .' in decasyllabic lines, but all the other poems written before the conversion are in shorter, quicker rhythms, 'La bise se rue . . .' (III xi) and 'Gaspard Hauser chante' (III iv) in octosyllabic lines, 'Le ciel est, par-dessus le toit . . .' in a combination of eight and four syllable lines, and four poems in 'vers impairs' of varying lengths, 'Tournez, tournez, bons chevaux de bois . . .' (III xvii) in nine syllable lines, 'Du fond du grabat . . .' (III ii) and 'Un grand sommeil noir . . .' in five syllable lines and 'Je ne sais pourquoi . . .' in a unique combination of five, thirteen and nine syllable lines. It should be noted that it was at about this time that Verlaine wrote, in April 1874, his 'Art poétique', later included in *Jadis et Naguère*, with its well-known opening stanza advocating the use of the 'vers impair':

> De la musique avant toute chose,
> Et pour cela préfère l'Impair
> Plus vague et plus soluble dans l'air,
> Sans rien en lui qui pèse ou qui pose.

Verlaine's return to the church however seems to have been accompanied by a return to a more conventional versification. The celebrated dialogue between the poet and God, 'Mon Dieu m'a dit . . .' (II iv), is in the form of ten sonnets in alexandrines although, as pointed out in the notes to the poem, there is such an extensive use of *enjambement* and the *caesura* is so frequently displaced or even abolished altogether that it is as if Verlaine feels unable as yet to make a wholehearted return to traditional techniques. This is also true, in a rather different way, of 'Parfums, couleurs, systèmes, lois . . .' (III viiii), written shortly afterwards towards the end of 1874, which is in the form of a sonnet, but an inverted sonnet with the tercets preceding the quatrains. Verlaine still continued to show a fondness for unusual rhythms and original rhyme schemes during the early part of the summer of 1875 at Stickney where he wrote 'L'échelonnement des haies . . .' (III xiii) in 'vers impairs' of seven syllables and 'Voix de l'Orgueil . . .' (I xix) which, although in alexandrines, has a complex rhyme scheme in which the last part of the first line of each verse is repeated in the fourth line of each verse, with these two lines rhyming with the second line, while the third line rhymes with the first, second and fourth lines in the following verse—a highly original variation on the *terza rima* system. 'Bon chevalier masqué . . .' (I i), also written in the summer of 1875 at Stickney, though again in alexandrines, has a slightly unusual touch in that it is in rhyming couplets while 'J'avais peiné comme Sisyphe . . .' (I ii), written in September 1875, is in octosyllabic lines and in *terza rima* form.

But it was in fact at this time, in the late summer of 1875, when Verlaine had a tremendous burst of poetic activity while on holiday in France, that he abandoned the last vestiges of his liking for unusual rhyme schemes and rhythmic patterns and returned completely to conventional forms. Almost all the poems written during these months—the two long poems involving Rimbaud, 'Qu'en dis-tu voyageur . . .' (I iii) and 'Malheureux, tous les dons . . .' (I iv), five of the six sonnets which follow them, the sonnet 'Vous voilà, vous voilà, pauvres bonnes pensées . . .' (III xii) and 'Je ne veux plus aimer que ma mère Marie . . .' (II ii)—are in alexandrines and from that date on Verlaine practised only rarely the unconventional kind of versification that had been such a feature of *Romances sans Paroles*. It is significant in this respect that, of the ten poems in 'vers impairs' in *Sagesse* at least seven were written before the end of 1875. In certain special circumstances however Verlaine could still be tempted by unusual techniques and in two of the poems addressed to his wife Mathilde in 1878 he used exclusively feminine rhymes to give a note of gentleness and it was no doubt for a similar reason that he also used exclusively feminine rhymes in the poem he wrote in 1879 on the death of the twenty-three-year-old son of Napoléon III, 'Prince mort en soldat . . .' (I xiii).

Along with this virtual abandonment of unusual rhythmic patterns and unconventional rhyme schemes the poems of *Sagesse* also exchange the twilight atmosphere that characterises the earliest of them for a much lighter tone in the later poems. Again it is the conversion that marks the watershed between the two kinds of imagery and it is perfectly understandable that, with his new found stability and certainty, Verlaine's poetry should have become bathed in sunlight rather than remain shadowed and overcast as it had been before. 'Bon chevalier masqué . . .' (I i), 'O vous comme un qui boite au loin . . .' (I vi), 'L'échelonnement des haies . . .' (III xiiii) 'La mer est plus belle . . .' (III xv) and 'C'est la fête du blé . . .' (III xxi) are typical of this lighter tonality and are in sharp contrast to the darker atmosphere of 'Le son du cor . . .' (III ix), 'Je ne sais pourquoi . . .' (III viii), 'Un grand sommeil noir . . .' (III v) and 'L'espoir luit . . .' (III iii).

A third change which comes over the poems of *Sagesse* written after the conversion is that Verlaine tends to lapse all too often into the laboriously descriptive kind of verse that he had practised on a previous occasion in *La Bonne Chanson* when he had also seen clearly the path lying ahead of him and had described his hopes and his intentions with a wealth of painstaking detail. So long as he had been emotionally involved in his conversion his poetry had kept its authentic 'Verlainian' note. The sonnet sequence for example is founded on the constant repetition of the first commandment and the syntax is extremely simple as, for instance, in the opening quatrains where phrases are added one after the other in a seemingly spontaneous way, and as in the opening lines of the fourth and sixth sonnets where again there is an almost conversational tone. 'Beauté des femmes . . .' (I v) begins in a similar fashion, as if Verlaine was thinking aloud, while 'Bon chevalier masqué' (I i) has numerous repetitions which create a typically casual note—'mon vieux cœur' is repeated three times at irregular intervals in the opening couplets and is later echoed by 'tout un cœur pur et fier' and 'tout un cœur jeune et bon'. 'Les faux beaux jours . . .' (I vii) too has an uncomplicated syntax and characteristic repetitions such as 'les faux beaux jours ont lui tout le jour' and 'ils ont lui tout le jour', 'ma pauvre âme' and 'pauvre âme', 'le ciel tout bleu' and 'le ciel chanteur'. But as Verlaine's religious ardour cooled he tended to adopt an intellectual rather than an emotional approach and when he mixes politics with religion as in 'Petits amis . . .' (I xi), 'Vous voici promus petits amis . . .' (I xii) and 'Vous reviendrez bientôt . . .' (I xiv), or writes a patriotic piece such as 'Prince mort en soldat . . .' (I xiii) or pontificates about the virtues of Arras and the vices of the capital in 'Parisien mon frère . . .' (III xviii) his poetry gives the impression of being far more consciously composed and its air of artificiality makes it far less effective.

THE REPUTATION OF SAGESSE

This co-existence in the same volume of verse of two quite different kinds of poetry—on the one hand the kind which expounds a logical train of thought in conventional patterns of versification, and on the other the kind which conveys an undefined but deeply felt emotional state in verse forms more suited to the expression of feelings than ideas—has been increasingly recognized by recent critics of *Sagesse*. 'Ses faiblesses sont réelles, évidentes', writes Jacques Robichez (*Œuvres poétiques*, p. 173), 'mais il n'en reste pas moins que quelques-uns des chefs-d'œuvre de Verlaine se trouvent dans *Sagesse*'. Jacques Borel too considers that 'l'accent proprement verlainien de *Sagesse*' is to be found only in 'ces quelques poèmes écrits avant même que le recueil ne fût conçu' (*Œuvres poétiques complètes*, p. 234). Earlier critics, however, rated *Sagesse* more highly. Mallarmé, for example, when asked which were the best parts of Verlaine's work, replied, in his usual convoluted style: 'Tout, de loin ou de près, ce qui s'affilie à *Sagesse*, en dépend et pourrait y retourner pour grossir l'unique livre: là, en un instant principal, ayant écho par tout Verlaine, le doigt a été mis sur la touche inouie qui résonnera solitairement, séculairement) (Stéphane Mallarmé, *Œuvres complètes*, Gallimard, Bibliothèque de la Pléiade, 1951, p. 873).

But when Mallarmé made this assessment in 1896 the reputation of *Sagesse* and its author was secure. The situation had been very different fifteen years before when *Sagesse* was first published at Verlaine's own expense in an edition limited to 500 copies. The volume passed almost unnoticed in the press and received only a handful of reviews. Verlaine had been out of the usual literary circles for the previous eight years and this no doubt explained in a large measure the lack of interest in his latest work. But with the publication of his *Poètes maudits* in the magazine *Lutèce* in 1883 and its appearance in book form the following year at the same time as Huysmans' novel *A Rebours* where Verlaine is singled out as one of the major poets of the day, his reputation rapidly became established and a second, revised edition of *Sagesse* was published in 1889 and the volume was thereafter reprinted at regular intervals.

THE TEXT OF SAGESSE

Of these two slightly different editions, the original one of 1881 and the second edition of 1889, it is the original one that has been taken as the model for the present edition though the two poems introduced into the 1889 edition are given in the notes at the appropriate place. There also exist two manuscripts of *Sagesse*, the one which Verlaine prepared in 1880 for the original edition and which he then gave to Ernest Delahaye, and an earlier, slightly shorter one prepared in 1878 which he presented to his wife Mathilde. These manuscripts, along with that of *Cellulairement*, prepared in 1875, are sometimes useful in the difficult task of ascertaining the exact date of composition of the poems of *Sagesse*, as are, in a few cases, letters to various friends in which Verlaine enclosed copies of certain poems very soon after they were written. Mention must also be made of an annotated copy of the third edition of *Sagesse* in 1893 presented to Count Kessler by Verlaine, although the dates he attributes to his poems are often incorrect to a greater or lesser degree since at that time, after a lapse of between thirteen and twenty years, his recollection of where and when he had written his poems was by no means accurate.

SELECT BIBLIOGRAPHY

EDITIONS

Paul Verlaine, *Œuvres complètes* (2 vols.), introduction d'Octave Nadal, études et notes de Jacques Borel, Le club du meilleur livre, 1959–60.

Paul Verlaine, *Œuvres poétiques complètes*, texte établi et annoté par Y.-G. Le Dantec, édition révisée par Jacques Borel, Gallimard, Bibliothèque de la Pléiade, 1962.

Paul Verlaine, *Œuvres poétiques*, édition de Jacques Robichez, Garnier, 1969.

Paul Verlaine, *Sagesse*, edited by V. P. Underwood, Zwemmer, 1944.

Paul Verlaine, *Sagesse*, édition critique commentée par Louis Morice, Nizet, 1948.

Paul Verlaine, *Correspondance*, édition d'Ad. van Bever, Messein, 1922–9.

CRITICISM

Antoine Adam, *Verlaine*, Paris, Hatier 1953, new edition 1961, translated into English as *The Art of Paul Verlaine*, New York University Press, 1963.

J.-H. Bornecque, *Verlaine par lui-même*, Editions du Seuil, 1966.

A. E. Carter, *Verlaine, a study in parallels*, University of Toronto Press, 1965.

C. Chadwick, *Paul Verlaine*, The Athlone Press of the University of London, 1973.

Pierre Martino, *Verlaine*, Boivin, 1924, new edition, 1959.

Louis Morice, *Verlaine, le drame religieux*, Beauchesne, 1946.

François Porché, *Verlaine tel qu'il fut*, Flammaorin, 1933.

Joanna Richardson, *Verlaine*, Weidenfeld, 1971.

Jean Richer, *Paul Verlaine*, Seghers, Poètes d'aujourd'hui, 1953.

V. P. Underwood, *Verlaine et l'Angleterre*, Nizet, 1956.

Eléonore M. Zimmermann, *Magies de Verlaine*, Corti, 1967.

PAUL VERLAINE

SAGESSE

A MA MERE

PREFACE

L'auteur de ce livre n'a pas toujours pensé comme aujourd'hui. Il a longtemps erré dans la corruption contemporaine, y prenant sa part de faute et d'ignorance. Des chagrins très mérités l'ont depuis averti, et Dieu lui a fait la grâce de comprendre l'avertissement. Il s'est prosterné devant l'autel longtemps méconnu, il adore la Toute-Bonté et invoque la Toute-Puissance, fils soumis de l'Eglise, le dernier en mérites, mais plein de bonne volonté.

Le sentiment de sa faiblesse et le souvenir de ses chutes l'ont guidé dans l'élaboration de cet ouvrage qui est son premier acte de foi public depuis un long silence littéraire: on n'y trouvera rien, il l'espère, de contraire à cette charité que l'auteur, désormais chrétien, doit aux pécheurs dont il a jadis et presque naguère pratiqué les haïssables mœurs.

Deux ou trois pièces toutefois rompent le silence qu'il s'est en conscience imposé à cet égard, mais on observera qu'elles portent sur des actes publics, sur des événements dès lors trop généralement providentiels pour qu'on ne puisse voir dans leur énergie qu'un témoignage nécessaire, qu'une *confession* sollicitée par l'idée du devoir religieux et d'une espérance française.

L'auteur a publié très jeune, c'est-à-dire il y a une dizaine et une douzaine d'années, des vers sceptiques et tristement légers. Il ose compter qu'en ceux-ci nulle dissonance n'ira choquer la délicatesse d'une oreille catholique: ce serait sa plus chère gloire comme c'est son espoir le plus fier.

Paris, 30 juillet 1880

I

i

Bon chevalier masqué qui chevauche en silence,
Le Malheur a percé mon vieux cœur de sa lance.

Le sang de mon vieux cœur n'a fait qu'un jet vermeil,
Puis s'est évaporé sur les fleurs, au soleil. 4

L'ombre éteignit mes yeux, un cri vint à ma bouche,
Et mon vieux cœur est mort dans un frisson farouche.

Alors le chevalier Malheur s'est rapproché,
Il a mis pied à terre et sa main m'a touché. 8

Son doigt ganté de fer entra dans ma blessure
Tandis qu'il attestait sa loi d'une voix dure.

Et voici qu'au contact glacé du doigt de fer
Un cœur me renaissait, tout un cœur pur et fier. 12

Et voici que, fervent d'une candeur divine,
Tout un cœur jeune et bon battit dans ma poitrine.

Or, je restais tremblant, ivre, incrédule un peu,
Comme un homme qui voit des visions de Dieu. 16

Mais le bon chevalier, remonté sur sa bête,
En s'éloignant, me fit un signe de la tête

Et me cria (j'entends *encore* cette voix):
«Au moins, prudence! Car c'est bon pour une fois.» 20

ii

J'avais peiné comme Sisyphe
Et comme Hercule travaillé
Contre la Chair qui se rebiffe.   3

J'avais lutté, j'avais baillé
Des coups à trancher des montagnes,
Et comme Achille ferraillé.   6

Farouche ami qui m'accompagnes,
Tu le sais, courage païen,
Si nous en fimes, des campagnes,   9

Si nous avons négligé rien
Dans cette guerre exténuante,
Si nous avons travaillé bien!   12

Le tout en vain: l'âpre géante
A mon effort de tout côté
Opposait sa ruse ambiante,   15

Et toujours un lâche abrité
Dans mes conseils qu'il environne
Livrait les clefs de la cité.   18

Que ma chance fût male ou bonne,
Toujours un parti de mon cœur
Ouvrait sa porte à la Gorgone.   21

Toujours l'ennemi suborneur
Savait envelopper d'un piège
Même la victoire et l'honneur!   24

J'étais le vaincu qu'on assiège,
Prêt à vendre son sang bien cher,
Quand, blanche, en vêtements de neige,   27

Toute belle au front humble et fier,
Une Dame vint sur la nue,
Qui d'un signe fit fuir la Chair.   30

Dans une tempête inconnue
De rage et de cris inhumains,
Et déchirant sa gorge nue,   33

Le Monstre reprit ses chemins
Par les bois, pleins d'amours affreuses,
Et la Dame, joignant les mains :   36

—«Mon pauvre combattant qui creuses,
Dit-elle, ce dilemme en vain,
Trêve aux victoires malheureuses !   39

«Il t'arrive un secours divin
Dont je suis sûre messagère
Pour ton salut, possible enfin !»   42

—«O ma Dame dont la voix chère
Encourage un blessé jaloux
De voir finir l'atroce guerre,   45

«Vous qui parlez d'un ton si doux
En m'annonçant de bonnes choses,
Ma Dame, qui donc êtes-vous ?»   48

—«J'étais née avant toutes causes
Et je verrai la fin de tous
Les effets, étoiles et roses.   51

«En même temps, bonne, sur vous,
Hommes faibles et pauvres femmes,
Je pleure, et je vous trouve fous !   54

«Je pleure sur vos tristes âmes,
J'ai l'amour d'elles, j'ai la peur
D'elles et de leurs vœux infâmes !   57

«O ceci n'est pas le bonheur.
Veillez. Quelqu'un l'a dit que j'aime,
Veillez, crainte du suborneur !   60

«Veillez, crainte du jour suprême!
Qui je suis? me demandais-tu.
Mon nom courbe les anges même.   63

«Je suis le cœur de la vertu,
Je suis l'âme de la sagesse,
Mon nom brûle l'Enfer têtu,   66

«Je suis la douceur qui redresse,
J'aime tous et n'accuse aucun,
Mon nom, seul, se nomme promesse,   69

«Je suis l'unique hôte opportun,
Je parle au Roi le vrai langage
Du matin rose et du soir brun,   72

«Je suis la PRIÈRE, et mon gage
C'est ton vice en déroute au loin ;
Ma condition: «Toi, sois sage.»   75

—«Oui, ma Dame, et soyez témoin!»

iii

Qu'en dis-tu, voyageur, des pays et des gares ?
Du moins as-tu cueilli l'ennui, puisqu'il est mûr,
Toi que voilà fumant de maussades cigares,
Noir, projetant une ombre absurde sur le mur ?   4

Tes yeux sont aussi morts depuis les aventures,
Ta grimace est la même et ton deuil est pareil :
Telle la lune vue à travers des mâtures,
Telle la vieille mer sous le jeune soleil,   8

Tel l'ancien cimetière aux tombes toujours neuves !
Mais voyons, et dis-nous les récits devinés,
Ces désillusions pleurant le long des fleuves,
Ces dégoûts comme autant de fades nouveau-nés,   12

Ces femmes ! Dis les gaz, et l'horreur identique
Du mal toujours, du laid partout sur tes chemins,
Et dis l'Amour et dis encor la Politique,
Avec du sang déshonoré d'encre à leurs mains.   16

Et puis surtout ne va pas t'oublier toi-même,
Traînassant ta faiblesse et ta simplicité,
Partout où l'on bataille et partout où l'on aime,
D'une façon si triste et folle, en vérité !   20

A-t-on assez puni cette lourde innocence ?
Qu'en dis-tu ? L'homme est dur, mais la femme ? Et tes pleurs,
Qui les a bus ? Et quelle âme qui les recense
Console ce qu'on peut appeler tes malheurs ?   24

Ah les autres, ah, toi ! Crédule à qui te flatte,
Toi qui rêvais (c'était trop excessif aussi)
Je ne sais quelle mort légère et délicate !
Ah, toi, l'espèce d'ange avec ce vœu transi !   28

Mais maintenant les plans, les buts ? Es-tu de force,
Ou si d'avoir pleuré t'a détrempé le cœur ?
L'arbre est tendre s'il faut juger d'après l'écorce,
Et tes aspects ne sont pas ceux d'un grand vainqueur.   32

Si gauche encore ! avec l'aggravation d'être
Une sorte à présent d'idyllique engourdi
Qui surveille le ciel bête par la fenêtre
Ouverte aux yeux matois du démon de midi.   36

Si le même dans cette extrême décadence!
Enfin!—Mais à ta place un être avec du sens,
Payant les violons, voudrait mener la danse,
Au risque d'alarmer quelque peu les passants.   40

N'as-tu pas, en fouillant les recoins de ton âme,
Un beau vice à tirer comme un sabre au soleil,
Quelque vice joyeux, effronté, qui s'enflamme
Et vibre, et darde rouge au front du ciel vermeil?   44

Un ou plusieurs? Si oui, tant mieux! Et pars bien vite
En guerre, et bats d'estoc et de taille, sans choix
Surtout, et mets ce masque indolent où s'abrite
La haine inassouvie et repue à la fois . . .   48

Il faut n'être pas dupe en ce farceur de monde
Où le bonheur n'a rien d'exquis et d'alléchant
S'il n'y frétille un peu de pervers et d'immonde,
Et pour n'être pas dupe il faut être méchant.   52

—Sagesse humaine, ah! j'ai les yeux sur d'autres choses,
Et parmi ce passé dont ta voix décrivait
L'ennui, pour des conseils encore plus moroses,
Je ne me souviens plus que du mal que j'ai fait.   56

Dans tous les mouvements bizarres de ma vie,
De mes «malheurs», selon le moment et le lieu,
Des autres et de moi, de la route suivie,
Je n'ai rien retenu que la grâce de Dieu.   60

Si je me sens puni, c'est que je le dois être,
Ni l'homme ni la femme ici ne sont pour rien,
Mais j'ai le ferme espoir d'un jour pouvoir connaître
Le pardon et la paix promis à tout Chrétien.   64

Bien de n'être pas dupe en ce monde d'une heure,
Mais pour ne l'être pas durant l'éternité,
Ce qu'il faut à tout prix qui règne et qui demeure,
Ce n'est pas la méchanceté, c'est la bonté.   68

iv

Malheureux! Tous les dons, la gloire du baptême,
Ton enfance chrétienne, une mère qui t'aime,
La force et la santé comme le pain et l'eau,
Cet avenir enfin, décrit dans le tableau
De ce passé plus clair que le jeu des marées,   5
Tu pilles tout, tu perds en viles simagrées
Jusqu'aux derniers pouvoirs de ton esprit, hélas!
La malédiction de n'être jamais las,
Suit tes pas sur le monde où l'horizon t'attire,
L'enfant prodigue avec des gestes de satyre!   10
Nul avertissement, douloureux ou moqueur,
Ne prévaut sur l'élan funeste de ton cœur.
Tu flânes à travers péril et ridicule,
Avec l'irresponsable audace d'un Hercule
Dont les travaux seraient fous nécessairement.   15
L'amitié—dame!—a tu son reproche clément,
Et chaste, et sans aucun espoir que le suprême,
Vient prier, comme au lit d'un mourant qui blasphème.
La patrie oubliée est dure au fils affreux,
Et le monde alentour dresse ses buissons creux   20
Où ton désir mauvais s'épuise en flèches mortes.
Maintenant il te faut passer devant les portes
Hâtant le pas de peur qu'on ne lâche le chien,
Et si tu n'entends pas rire, c'est encor bien.
Malheureux, toi Français, toi Chrétien, quel dommage!   25
Mais tu vas, la pensée obscure de l'image
D'un bonheur qu'il te faut immédiat, étant
Athée (avec la foule!) et jaloux de l'instant,
Tout appétit parmi ces appétits féroces,
Épris de la fadaise actuelle, mots, noces   30
Et festins, «la Science», et «l'esprit de Paris»,
Tu vas magnifiant ce par quoi tu péris,
Imbécile! et niant le soleil qui t'aveugle!
Tout ce que les temps ont de bête paît et beugle
Dans ta cervelle, ainsi qu'un troupeau dans un pré,   35

Et les vices de tout le monde ont émigré
Pour ton sang dont le fer lâchement s'étiole.
Tu n'es plus bon à rien de propre, ta parole
Est morte de l'argot et du ricanement,
Et d'avoir rabâché les bourdes du moment,   40
Ta mémoire, de tant d'obscénités bondée,
Ne saurait accueillir la plus petite idée,
Et patauge parmi l'égoïsme ambiant,
En quête d'on ne peut dire quel vil néant!
Seul, entre les débris honnis de ton désastre,   45
L'Orgueil, qui met la flamme au front du poétastre
Et fait au criminel un prestige odieux,
Seul, l'Orgueil est vivant, il danse dans tes yeux,
Il regarde la Faute et rit de s'y complaire.
—Dieu des humbles, sauvez cet enfant de colère!   50

                              V

Beauté des femmes, leur faiblesse, et ces mains pâles
Qui font souvent le bien et peuvent tout le mal,
Et ces yeux, où plus rien ne reste d'animal
Que juste assez pour dire: «assez» aux fureurs mâles!   4

Et toujours, maternelle endormeuse des râles,
Même quand elle ment, cette voix! Matinal
Appel, ou chant bien doux à vêpre, ou frais signal,
Ou beau sanglot qui va mourir au pli des châles!...   8

Hommes durs! Vie atroce et laide d'ici-bas!
Ah! que du moins, loin des baisers et des combats,
Quelque chose demeure un peu sur la montagne,

Quelque chose du cœur enfantin et subtil,   12
Bonté, respect! Car qu'est-ce qui nous accompagne,
Et vraiment, quand la mort viendra, que reste-t-il?

vi

O vous, comme un qui boite au loin, Chagrins et Joies,
Toi, cœur saignant d'hier qui flambes aunourd'hui
C'est vrai pourtant, que c'est fini, que tout a fui
De nos sens aussi bien les ombres que les proies.   4

Vieux bonheurs, vieux malheurs, comme une file d'oies
Sur la route en poussière où tous les pieds ont lui,
Bon voyage! Et le Rire, et, plus vieille que lui,
Toi, Tristesse, noyée au vieux noir que tu broies!   8

Et les reste!—Un doux vide, un grand renoncement,
Quelqu'un en nous qui sent la paix immensément,
Une candeur d'une fraîcheur délicieuse . . .

Et voyez! notre cœur qui saignait sous l'orgueil,   1 2
Il flambe dans l'amour, et s'en va faire accueil
A la vie, en faveur d'une mort précieuse!

vii

Les faux beaux jours ont lui tout le jour, ma pauvre âme,
Et les voici vibrer aux cuivres du couchant.
Ferme les yeux, pauvre âme, et rentre sur-le-champ;
Une tentation des pires. Fuis l'Infâme.   4

Ils ont lui tout le jour en longs grêlons de flamme,
Battant toute vendange aux collines, couchant
Toute moisson de la vallée, et ravageant
Le ciel tout bleu, le ciel chanteur qui te réclame.   8

O pâlis, et va-t'en, lente et joignant les mains.
Si ces hiers allaient manger nos beaux demains?
Si la vieille folie était encore en route?

Ces souvenirs, va-t-il falloir les retuer?
Un assaut furieux, le suprême sans doute!
O, va prier contre l'orage, va prier.

viii

La vie humble aux travaux ennuyeux et faciles
Est une œuvre de choix qui veut beaucoup d'amour.
Rester gai quand le jour, triste, succède au jour,
Être fort, et s'user en circonstances viles,   4

N'entendre, n'écouter aux bruits des grandes villes
Que l'appel, ô mon Dieu, des cloches dans la tour,
Et faire un de ces bruits soi-même, cela pour
L'accomplissement vil de tâches puériles,   8

Dormir chez les pécheurs étant un pénitent;
N'aimer que le silence et converser pourtant;
Le temps si long dans la patience si grande,

Le scrupule naïf aux repentirs têtus,   12
Et tous ces soins autour de ces pauvres vertus!
—Fi, dit l'Ange Gardien, de l'orgueil qui marchande!

ix

Sagesse d'un Louis Racine, je t'envie!
O n'avoir pas suivi les leçons de Rollin,
N'être pas né dans le grand siècle à son déclin,
Quand le soleil couchant, si beau, dorait la vie,   4

Quand Maintenon jetait sur la France ravie
L'ombre douce et la paix de ses coiffes de lin,
Et royale abritait la veuve et l'orphelin,
Quand l'étude de la prière était suivie,   8

Quand poète et docteur, simplement, bonnement,
Communiaient avec des ferveurs de novices,
Humbles servaient la Messe et chantaient aux offices,

Et le printemps venu, prenaient un soin charmant   12
D'aller dans les Auteuils cueillir lilas et roses
En louant Dieu, comme Garo, de toutes choses!

x

Non. Il fut gallican, ce siècle, et janséniste!
C'est vers le Moyen Age, énorme et délicat,
Qu'il faudrait que mon cœur en panne naviguât,
Loin de nos jours d'esprit charnel et de chair triste.   4

Roi, politicien, moine, artisan, chimiste,
Architecte, soldat, médecin, avocat,
Quel temps! Oui, que mon cœur naufragé rembarquât
Pour toute cette force ardente, souple, artiste!   8

Et là que j'eusse part—quelconque, chez les rois
Ou bien ailleurs, n'importe,—à la chose vitale,
Et que je fusse un saint, actes bons, pensers droits,

Haute théologie et solide morale,   12
Guidé par la folie unique de la Croix
Sur tes ailes de pierre, ô folle Cathédrale!

xi

Petits amis qui sûtes nous prouver
Par A plus B que deux et deux font quatre,
Mais qui depuis voulez parachever
Une victoire où l'on se laissait battre,   4

Et couronner vos conquêtes d'un coup
Par ce soufflet à la mémoire humaine:
«Dieu ne nous a révélé rien du tout,
Car nous disons qu'il n'est que l'ombre vaine,   8

Que le profil et que l'allongement,
Sur tous les murs que la peur édifie,
De votre pur et simple mouvement,
Et nous dictons cette philosophie!»   12

—Frères trop chers, laissez-nous rire un peu,
Nous les fervents d'une logique rance,
Qui justement n'avons de foi qu'en Dieu
Et mettons notre espoir dans l'Espérance,   16

Laissez-nous rire un peu, pleurer aussi,
Pleurer sur vous, rire du vieux blasphème,
Rire du vieux Satan stupide ainsi,
Pleurer sur cet Adam dupe quand même!   20

Frères de nous qui payons vos orgueils,
Tous fils du même Amour, ah! la science,
Allons donc, allez donc, c'est nos cercueils
Naïfs ou non, c'est notre méfiance   24

Ou notre confiance aux seuls Récits,
C'est notre oreille ouverte toute grande
Ou tristement fermée au Mot précis!
Frères, lâchez la science gourmande   28

Qui veut voler sur des ceps défendus
Le fruit sanglant qu'il ne faut pas connaître.
Lâchez son bras qui vous tient attendus
Pour des enfers que Dieu n'a pas fait naître,   32

Mais qui sont l'œuvre affreuse du péché,
Car nous, les fils attentifs de l'Histoire,
Nous tenons pour l'honneur jamais taché,
De la Tradition, supplice et gloire!   36

Nous sommes surs des Aïeux nous disant
Qu'ils ont vu Dieu sous telle ou telle forme,
Et prédisant aux crimes d'à *présent*
La peine immense ou le pardon énorme.   40

Puisqu'ils avaient vu Dieu présent toujours,
Puisqu'ils ne mentaient pas, puisque nos crimes
Vont effrayants, puisque vos yeux sont courts,
Et puisqu'il est des repentirs sublimes,   44

Ils ont dit tout. Savoir le reste est bien,
Que deux et deux fassent quatre, à merveille!
Riens innocents, mais des riens moins que rien,
La dernière heure étant là qui surveille   48

Tout autre soin dans l'homme en vérité!
Gardez que trop chercher ne vous séduise
Loin d'une sage et forte humilité . . .
Le seul savant, c'est encore Moïse.   52

xii

Or, vous voici promus, petits amis,
Depuis les temps de ma lettre première,
Promus, disais-je, aux fiers emplois promis
A votre thèse, en ces jours de lumière.   4

Vous voici rois de France! A votre tour!
(Rois à plusieurs d'une France postiche,
Mais rois de fait et non sans quelque amour
D'un trône lourd avec un budget riche.)   8

A l'œuvre, petits amis! Nous avons droit
De vous y voir, payant de notre poche,
Et d'être un peu réjouis à l'endroit
De votre état sans peur et sans reproche.   12

Sans peur? Du maître? O le maître, mais c'est
L'Ignorant-chiffre et le Suffrage-nombre,
Total, le peuple, «un âne» fort «qui s'est
Cabré», pour vous, espoir clair, puis fait sombre,   16

Cabré comme une chèvre, c'est le mot.
Et votre bras, saignant jusqu'à l'aisselle,
S'efforce en vain: fort comme Béhémot,
Le monstre tire . . . et votre peur est telle   20

Que l'âne brait, que le voilà parti
Qui par les dents vous boute cent ruades
En forme de reproche bien senti . . .
Courez après, frottant vos reins malades!   24

O Peuple, nous t'aimons immensément:
N'es-tu donc pas la pauvre âme ignorante
En proie à tout ce qui sait et qui ment?
N'es-tu donc pas l'immensité souffrante?   28

La charité nous fait chercher tes maux,
La foi nous guide à travers tes ténèbres.
On t'a rendu semblable aux animaux,
Moins leur candeur, et plein d'instincts funèbres.   32

L'orgueil t'a pris en ce quatre-vingt-neuf,
Nabuchodonosor, et te fait paître,
Ane obstiné, mouton buté, dur bœuf,
Broutant pouvoir, famille, soldat, prêtre!   36

O paysan cassé sur tes sillons,
Pâle ouvrier qu'esquinte la machine,
Membres sacrés de Jésus-Christ, allons,
Relevez-vous, honorez votre échine,   40

Portez l'amour qu'il faut à vos bras forts,
Vos pieds vaillants sont les plus beaux du monde,
Respectez-les, fuyez ces chemins tors,
Fermez l'oreille à ce conseil immonde,   44

Redevenez les Français d'autrefois
Fils de l'Eglise, et dignes de vos pères!
O s'ils savaient ceux-ci sur vos pavois,
Leurs os sueraient de honte aux cimetières.   48

—Vous, nos tyrans minuscules d'un jour,
(L'énormité des actes rend les princes
Surtout de souche impure, et malgré cour
Et splendeur et le faste, encor plus minces)   52

Laissez le règne et rentrez dans le rang.
Aussi bien l'heure est proche où la tourmente
Vous va donner des loisirs, et tout blanc
L'avenir flotte avec sa Fleur charmante   56

Sur la Bastille absurde où vos teniez
La France aux fers d'un blasphème et d'un schisme,
Et la chronique en de cléments Téniers
Déjà vous peint allant au catéchisme.   60

xiii

Prince mort en soldat à cause de la France,
        Ame certes élue,
Fier jeune homme si pur tombé plein d'espérance,
        Je t'aime et te salue!   4

Ce monde est si mauvais, notre pauvre patrie
        Va sous tant de ténèbres,
Vaisseau désemparé dont l'équipage crie
        Avec des voix funèbres,   8

Ce siècle est un tel ciel tragique où les naufrages
        Semblent écrits d'avance . . .
Ma jeunesse, élevée aux doctrines sauvages,
        Détesta ton enfance,   12

Et plus tard, cœur pirate épris des seules côtes
        Où la révolte naisse,
Mon âge d'homme, noir d'orages et de fautes,
        Abhorrait ta jeunesse.   16

Maintenant j'aime Dieu, dont l'amour et la foudre
        M'ont fait une âme neuve,
Et maintenant que mon orgueil réduit en poudre,
        Humble, accepte l'épreuve,   20

J'admire ton destin, j'adore, tout en larmes
        Pour les pleurs de ta mère,
Dieu qui te fit mourir, beau prince, sous les armes,
        Comme un héros d'Homère.   24

Et je dis, réservant d'ailleurs mon vœu suprême
        Au lys de Louis Seize:
Napoléon, qui fus digne du diadème,
        Gloire à ta mort française!   28

Et priez bien pour nous, pour cette France ancienne,
        Aujourd'hui vraiment «Sire»,
Dieu qui vous couronna, sur la terre païenne,
        Bon chrétien, du martyre!   32

xiv

Vous reviendrez bientôt, les bras pleins de pardons,
        Selon votre coutume,
O Pères excellents qu'aujourd'hui nous perdons
        Pour comble d'amertume.   4

Vous reviendrez, vieillards exquis, avec l'honneur,
        Et sa règle chérie,
Et que de pleurs joyeux, et quels cris de bonheur
        Dans toute la patrie!   8

Vous reviendrez, après ces glorieux exils,
        Après des moissons d'âmes,
Après avoir prié pour ceux-ci, fussent-ils
        Encore plus infâmes,   12

Après avoir couvert les îles et la mer
    De votre ombre si douce
Et réjoui le ciel et consterné l'enfer,
    Béni qui vous repousse,   16

Béni qui vous dépouille au cri de liberté,
    Béni l'impie en armes,
Et l'enfant qu'il vous prend des bras,—et racheté
    Nos crimes par vos larmes!   20

Proscrits des jours, vainqueurs des temps, non point adieu,
    Vous êtes l'espérance.
A tantôt, Pères saints, qui nous vaudrez de Dieu
    Le salut pour la France!   24

XV

On n'offense que Dieu qui seul pardonne.
                         Mais
On constriste son frère, on l'afflige, on le blesse,
On fait gronder sa haine ou pleurer sa faiblesse,   3
Et c'est un crime affreux qui va troubler la paix
Des simples, et donner au monde sa pâture,
Scandale, cœurs perdus, gros mots et rire épais.   6

Le plus souvent, par un effet de la nature
Des choses, ce péché trouve son châtiment
Même ici-bas, féroce et long, communément.   9
Mais l'*Amour* tout-puissant donne à la créaure
Le sens de son malheur, qui mène au repentir
Par une route lente et haute, mais très sûre.   12

Alors un grand désir, un seul, vient investir
Le pénitent, après les premières alarmes,
Et c'est d'humilier son front devant les larmes   15
De naguère, sans rien qui pourrait amortir
Le coup droit pour l'orgueil, et de rendre les armes
Comme un soldat vaincu,—triste, de bonne foi.   18

O ma sœur qui m'avez puni, pardonnez-moi!

xvi

Ecoutez la chanson bien douce
Qui ne pleure que pour vous plaire.
Elle est discrète, elle est légère:
Un frisson d'eau sur de la mousse! 4

La voix vous fut connue (et chère?)
Mais à présent elle est voilée
Comme une veuve désolée,
Pourtant comme elle encore fière, 8

Et dans les longs plis de son voile
Qui palpite aux brises d'automne,
Cache et montre au cœur qui s'étonne
La vérité comme une étoile. 12

Elle dit, la voix reconnue,
Que la bonté c'est notre vie,
Que de la haine et de l'envie
Rien ne reste, la mort venue. 16

Elle parle aussi de la gloire
D'être simple sans plus attendre,
Et de noces d'or et du tendre
Bonheur d'une paix sans victoire. 20

Accueillez la voix qui persiste
Dans son naïf épithalame.
Allez, rien n'est meilleur à l'âme
Que de faire une âme moins triste! 24

Elle est *en peine* et *de passage*,
L'âme qui souffre sans colère,
Et comme sa morale est claire!...
Ecoutez la chanson bien sage. 28

xvii

Les chères mains qui furent miennes,
Toutes petites, toutes belles,
Après ces méprises mortelles
Et toutes ces choses paiennes,   4

Après les rades et les grèves,
Et les pays et les provinces,
Royales mieux qu'au temps des princes
Les chères mains m'ouvrent les rêves.   8

Mains en songe, mains sur mon âme,
Sais-je, moi, ce que vous daignâtes,
Parmi ces rumeurs scélérates,
Dire à cette âme qui se pâme?   12

Ment-elle, ma vision chaste
D'affinité spirituelle,
De complicité maternelle,
D'affection étroite et vaste?   16

Remords si cher, peine très bonne,
Rêves bénis, mains consacrées,
O ces mains, ses mains vénérées,
Faites le geste qui pardonne!   20

xviii

Et j'ai revu l'enfant unique: il m'a semblé
Que s'ouvrait dans mon cœur la dernière blessure,
Celle dont la douleur plus exquise m'assure
D'une mort désirable en un jour consolé.   4

La bonne flèche aiguë et sa fraicheur qui dure!
En ces instants choisis elles ont éveillé
Les rêves un peu lourds du scrupule ennuyé,
Et tout mon sang chrétien chanta la Chanson pure. 8

J'entends encor, je vois encor! Loi du devoir
Si douce! Enfin je sais ce qu'est entendre et voir,
J'entends, je vois toujours! Voix des bonnes pensées!

Innocence, avenir! Sage et silencieux,   12
Que je vais vous aimer, vous un instant pressées,
Belles petites mains qui fermerez nos yeux!

xix

Voix de l'Orgueil: un cri puissant comme d'un cor,
Des étoiles de sang sur des cuirasses d'or;
On trébuche à travers des chaleurs d'incendie . . .
Mais en somme la voix s'en va, comme d'un cor.   4

Voix de la Haine: cloche en mer, fausse, assourdie
De neige lente. Il fait si froid! Lourde, affadie,
La vie a peur et court follement sur le quai
Loin de la cloche qui devient plus assourdie.   8

Voix de la Chair: un gros tapage fatigué.
Des gens ont bu. L'endroit fait semblant d'être gai.
Des yeux, des noms, et l'air plein de parfums atroces
Où vient mourir le gros tapage fatigué.   12

Voix d'Autrui: des lointains dans les brouillards. Des noces
Vont et viennent. Des tas d'embarras. Des négoces,
Et tout le cirque des civilisations
Au son trotte-menu du violon des noces.   16

Colères, soupirs noirs, regrets, tentations
Qu'il a fallu pourtant que nous entendissions
Pour l'assourdissement des silences honnêtes,
Colères, soupirs noirs, regrets, tentations,   20

Ah! les Voix, mourez donc, mourantes que vous êtes,
Sentences, mots en vain, métaphores mal faites,
Toute la rhétorique en fuite des péchés,
Ah! les Voix, mourez donc, mourantes que vous êtes! 24

Nous ne sommes plus ceux que vous auriez cherchés.
Mourez à nous, mourez aux humbles vœux cachés
Que nourrit la douceur de la Parole forte,
Car notre cœur n'est plus de ceux que vous cherchez!   28

Mourez parmi la voix que la prière emporte
Au ciel, dont elle seule ouvre et ferme la porte
Et dont elle tiendra les sceaux au dernier jour,
Mourez parmi la voix que la prière apporte,   32

Mourez parmi la voix terrible de l'Amour!

XX

L'ennemi se déguise en l'Ennui
Et me dit: «A quoi bon, pauvre dupe?»
Moi je passe et me moque de lui.   3
L'ennemi se déguise en la Chair
Et me dit: «Bah, bah, vive une jupe!»
Moi j'écarte le conseil amer.   6

L'ennemi se transforme en un Ange
De lumière et dit: «Qu'est ton effort
A côté des tributs de louange   9
Et de Foi dus au Père céleste?
Ton amour va-t-il jusqu'à la mort?»
Je réponds: «L'Espérance me reste.»   12

Comme c'est le vieux logicien,
Il a fait bientôt de me réduire
A ne plus *vouloir* répliquer rien,   15
Mais sachant *qui c'est*, épouvanté
De ne plus sentir les mondes luire,
Je prierai pour de l'humilité.   18

xxi

Va ton chemin sans plus t'inquiéter!
La route est droite et tu n'as qu'à monter,
Portant d'ailleurs le seul trésor qui vaille,
Et l'arme unique au cas d'une bataille :
La pauvreté d'esprit et Dieu pour toi.   5

Surtout il faut garder toute espérance.
Qu'importe un peu de nuit et de souffrance ?
La route est bonne et la mort est au bout.
Oui, garde toute espérance surtout.
La mort là-bas te dresse un lit de joie.   10

Et fais-toi doux de toute la douceur.
La vie est laide, encore c'est ta sœur.
Simple, gravis la côte et même chante,
Pour écarter la prudence méchante
Dont la voix basse est pour tenter ta foi.   15

Simple comme un enfant, gravis la côte,
Humble comme un pécheur qui hait la faute,
Chante, et même sois gai, pour défier
L'ennui que l'ennemi peut t'envoyer
Afin que tu t'endormes sur la voie.   20

Ris du vieux piège et du vieux séducteur,
Puisque la Paix est là, sur la hauteur,
Qui luit parmi des fanfares de gloire.
Monte, ravi, dans la nuit blanche et noire.
Déja l'Ange Gardien étend sur toi   25

Joyeusement des ailes de victoire.

xxii

Pourquoi triste, ô mon âme,
Triste jusqu'à la mort,
Quand l'effort te réclame,
Quand le suprême effort
Est là qui te réclame ?   5

Ah! tes mains que tu tords
Au lieu d'être à la tâche,
Tes lèvres que tu mords
Et leur silence lâche,
Et tes yeux qui sont morts !   10

N'as-tu pas l'espérance
De la fidélité,
Et, pour plus d'assurance
Dans la sécurité,
N'as-tu pas la souffrance ?   15

Mais chasse le sommeil
Et ce rêve qui pleure.
Grand jour et plein soleil !
Vois, il est plus que l'heure :
Le ciel bruit, vermeil,   20

Et la lumière crue,
Découpant d'un trait noir
Toute chose apparue,
Te montre le Devoir
Et sa forme bourrue.   25

Marche à lui vivement,
Tu verras disparaître
Tout aspect inclément
De sa manière d'être,
Avec l'éloignement.   30

C'est le dépositaire
Qui te garde un trésor
D'amour et de mystère,
Plus précieux que l'or,
Plus sûr que rien sur terre.   35

Les biens qu'on ne voit pas,
Toute joie inouïe,
Votre paix, saints combats,
L'extase épanouie
Et l'oubli d'ici-bas,   40
Et l'oubli d'ici-bas!

xxiii

Né l'enfant des grandes villes
Et des révoltes serviles,
J'ai là tout cherché, trouvé,
De tout appétit rêvé.
Mais, puisque rien n'en demeure,   5

J'ai dit un adieu léger
A tout ce qui peut changer,
Au plaisir, au bonheur même,
Et même à tout ce que j'aime
Hors de vous, mon doux Seigneur!   10

La Croix m'a pris sur ses ailes
Qui m'emporte aux meilleurs zèles,
Silence, expiation,
Et l'âpre vocation
Pour la vertu qui s'ignore.   15

Douce, chère Humilité!
Arrose ma charité,
Trempe-la de tes eaux vives,
O mon cœur, que tu ne vives
Qu'aux fins d'une bonne mort!   20

xxiv

L'âme antique était rude et vaine
Et ne voyait dans la douleur
Que l'acuité de la peine
Ou l'étonnement du malheur. 4

L'art, sa figure la plus claire,
Traduit ce double sentiment
Par deux grands types de la Mère
En proie au suprême tourment. 8

C'est la vieille reine de Troie:
Tous ses fils sont morts par le fer.
Alors ce deuil brutal aboie
Et glapit au bord de la mer. 12

Elle court le long du rivage,
Bavant vers le flot écumant,
Hirsute, criarde, sauvage,
La chienne littéralement!... 16

Et c'est Niobé, qui s'effare
Et garde fixement des yeux
Sur les dalles de pierre rare
Ses enfants tués par les dieux. 20

Le souffle expire sur sa bouche,
Elle meurt dans un geste fou.
Ce n'est plus qu'un marbre farouche
Là transporté nul ne sait d'où!... 24

La douleur chrétienne est immense,
Elle, comme le cœur humain.
Elle souffre, puis elle pense,
Et calme poursuit son chemin. 28

Elle est debout sur le Calvaire
Pleine de larmes et sans cris.
C'est également une mère,
Mais quelle mère de quel fils !   32

Elle participe au Supplice
Qui sauve toute nation,
Attendrissant le sacrifice
Par sa vaste compassion.   36

Et comme tous sont les fils d'elle,
Sur le monde et sur sa langueur
Tout la charité ruisselle
Des sept blessures de son cœur.   40

Au jour qu'il faudra, pour la gloire
Des cieux enfin tout grands ouverts,
Ceux qui surent et purent croire,
Bons et doux, sauf au seul Pervers,   44

Ceux-là, vers la joie infinie
Sur la colline de Sion,
Monteront d'une aile bénie
Aux plis de son assomption.   48

II

i

O mon Dieu, vous m'avez blessé d'amour
Et la blessure est encore vibrante,
O mon Dieu, vous m'avez blessé d'amour.   3

O mon Dieu, votre crainte m'a frappé
Et la brûlure est encor là qui tonne,
O mon Dieu, votre crainte m'a frappé.   6

O mon Dieu, j'ai connu que tout est vil
Et votre gloire en moi s'est installée,
O mon Dieu, j'ai connu que tout est vil.   9

Noyez mon âme aux flots de votre Vin.
Fondez ma vie au Pain de votre table,
Noyez mon âme aux flots de votre Vin.   12

Voici mon sang que je n'ai pas versé,
Voici ma chair indigne de souffrance,
Voici mon sang que je n'ai pas versé.   15

Voici mon front qui n'a pu que rougir,
Pour l'escabeau de vos pieds adorables,
Voici mon front qui n'a pu que rougir.   18

Voici mes mains qui n'ont pas travaillé,
Pour les charbons ardents et l'encens rare,
Voici mes mains qui n'ont pas travaillé.   21

Voici mon cœur qui n'a battu qu'en vain,
Pour palpiter aux ronces du Calvaire,
Voici mon cœur qui n'a battu qu'en vain.   24

Voici mes pieds, frivoles voyageurs,
Pour accourir au cri de votre grâce,
Voici mes pieds, frivoles voyageurs.   27

Voici ma voix, bruit maussade et menteur,
Pour les reproches de la Pénitence,
Voici ma voix, bruit maussade et menteur.   30

Voici mes yeux, luminaires d'erreur,
Pour être éteints aux pleurs de la prière,
Voici mes yeux, luminaires d'erreur.   33

Hélas, Vous, Dieu d'offrande et de pardon,
Quel est le puits de mon ingratitude,
Hélas, Vous, Dieu d'offrande et de pardon,   36

Dieu de terreur et Dieu de sainteté,
Hélas! ce noir abîme de mon crime,
Dieu de terreur et Dieu de sainteté,   39

Vous, Dieu de paix, de joie et de bonheur,
Toutes mes peurs, toutes mes ignorances,
Vous, Dieu de paix, de joie et de bonheur,   42

Vous connaissez tout cela, tout cela,
Et que je suis plus pauvre que personne,
Vous connaissez tout cela, tout cela,   45

Mais ce que j'ai, mon Dieu, je vous le donne.

ii

Je ne veux plus aimer que ma mère Marie.
Tous les autres amours sont de commandement.
Nécessaires qu'ils sont, ma mère seulement
Pourra les allumer aux cœurs qui l'ont chérie.   4

C'est pour Elle qu'il faut chérir mes ennemis,
C'est par Elle que j'ai voué ce sacrifice,
Et la douceur de cœur et le zèle au service,
Comme je la priais, Elle les a permis.   8

Et comme j'étais faible et bien méchant encore,
Aux mains lâches, les yeux éblouis des chemins,
Elle baissa mes yeux et me joignit les mains,
Et m'enseigna les mots par lesquels on adore.   12

C'est par Elle que j'ai voulu de ces chagrins,
C'est pour Elle que j'ai mon cœur dans les Cinq Plaies,
Et tous ces bons efforts vers les croix et les claies,
Comme je l'invoquais, Elle en ceignit mes reins.   16

Je ne veux plus penser qu'à ma mère Marie,
Siège de la Sagesse et source des pardons,
Mère de France aussi, de qui nous attendons
Inébranlablement l'honneur de la patrie.   20

Marie Immaculée, amour essentiel.
Logique de la foi cordiale et vivace,
En vous aimant qu'est-il de bon que je ne fasse,
En vous aimant du seul amour, Porte du ciel?   24

iii

Vous êtes calme, vous voulez un vœu discret,
Des secrets à mi-voix dans l'ombre et le silence,
Le cœur qui se répand plutôt qu'il ne s'élance,
Et ces timides, moins transis qu'il ne paraît.   4

Vous accueillez d'un geste exquis telles pensées
Qui ne marchent qu'en ordre et font le moins de bruit.
Votre main, toujours prête à la chute du fruit,
Patiente avec l'arbre et s'abstient de poussées.   8

Et si l'immense amour de vos commandements
Embrasse et presse tous en sa sollicitude,
Vos conseils vont dicter aux meilleurs et l'étude
Et le travail des plus humbles recueillements.   12

Le pécheur, s'il prétend vous connaître et vous plaire,
O vous qui nous aimant si fort parliez si peu,
Doit et peut, à tout temps du jour comme en tout lieu,
Bien faire obscurément son devoir et se taire,   16

Se taire pour le monde, un pur sénat de fous,
Se taire sur autrui, des âmes précieuses,
Car nous taire vous plaît, même aux heures pieuses,
Même à la mort, sinon devant le prêtre et vous.   20

Donnez-leur le silence et l'amour du mystère,
O Dieu glorifieur du bien fait en secret,
A ces timides moins transis qu'il ne paraît,
Et l'horreur, et le pli des choses de la terre.   24

Donnez-leur, ô mon Dieu, la résignation,
Toute forte douceur, l'ordre et l'intelligence,
Afin qu'au jour suprême ils gagnent l'indulgence
De l'Agneau formidable en la neuve Sion,   28

Afin qu'ils puissent dire: «Au moins nous sûmes croire»
Et que l'Agneau terrible, ayant tout supputé,
Leur réponde: «Venez, vous avez mérité,
Pacifiques, ma paix, et douloureux, ma gloire.»   32

iv

(i)

Mon Dieu m'a dit: Mon fils il faut m'aimer. Tu vois
Mon flanc percé, mon cœur qui rayonne et qui saigne,
Et mes pieds offensés que Madeleine baigne
De larmes, et mes bras douloureux sous le poids   4

De tes péchés, et mes mains ! Et tu vois la croix,
Tu vois les clous, le fiel, l'éponge, et tout t'enseigne
A n'aimer, en ce monde amer où la chair règne,
Que ma Chair et mon Sang, ma parole et ma voix.   8

Ne t'ai-je pas aimé jusqu'à la mort moi-même,
O mon frère en mon Père, ô mon fils en l'Esprit,
Et n'ai-je pas souffert, comme c'était écrit ?

N'ai-je pas sangloté ton angoisse suprême   12
Et n'ai-je pas sué la sueur de tes nuits,
Lamentable ami qui me cherches où je suis ?

(ii)

J'ai répondu : Seigneur, vous avez dit mon âme.
C'est vrai que je vous cherche et ne vous trouve pas.
Mais vous aimer ! Voyez comme je suis en bas,
Vous dont l'amour toujours monte comme la flamme.   4

Vous, la source de paix que toute soif réclame,
Hélas ! voyez un peu tous mes tristes combats !
Oserai-je adorer la trace de vos pas,
Sur ces genoux saignants d'un rampement infâme ?   8

Et pourtant je vous cherche en longs tâtonnements,
Je voudrais que votre ombre au moins vêtît ma honte,
Mais vous n'avez pas d'ombre, ô vous dont l'amour monte,

O vous, fontaine calme, amère aux seuls amants   12
De leur damnation, ô vous, toute lumière,
Sauf aux yeux dont un lourd baiser tient la paupière !

(iii)

—Il faut m'aimer ! Je suis l'universel Baiser,
Je suis cette paupière et je suis cette lèvre
Dont tu parles, ô chere malade, et cette fièvre,
Qui t'agite, c'est moi toujours ! Il faut oser   4

M'aimer! Oui, mon amour monte sans biaiser
Jusqu'où ne grimpe pas ton pauvre amour de chèvre,
Et t'emportera, comme un aigle vole un lièvre,
Vers des serpolets qu'un ciel cher vient arroser!   8

O ma nuit claire! ô tes yeux dans mon clair de lune!
O ce lit de lumière et d'eau parmi la brune!
Toute cette innocence et tout ce reposoir!

Aime-moi! Ces deux mots sont mes verbes suprêmes,   12
Car étant ton Dieu tout-puissant, je peux vouloir,
Mais je ne veux d'abord que pouvoir que tu m'aimes.

(iv)

Seigneur, c'est trop! Vraiment je n'ose. Aimer qui? Vous?
O! non! Je tremble et n'ose. O vous aimer, je n'ose,
Je ne veux pas! je suis indigne. Vous, la Rose   4
Immense des purs vents de l'Amour, ô Vous, tous

Les cœurs des saints, ô Vous qui fûtes le Jaloux
D'Israël, Vous, la chaste abeille qui se pose
Sur la seule fleur d'une innocence mi-close,
Quoi, *moi, moi*, pouvoir *Vous* aimer. Etes-vous fous,[1]   8

Père, Fils, Esprit? Moi ce pécheur-ci, ce lâche,
Ce superbe, qui fait le mal comme sa tâche
Et n'a dans tous ses sens, odorat, toucher, goût,

Vue, ouïe, et dans tout son être—hélas! dans tout   12
Son espoir et dans tout son remords, que l'extase
D'une caresse où le seul vieil Adam s'embrase?

[1] St. Augustin

(v)

Il faut m'aimer. Je suis Ces Fous que tu nommais,
Je suis l'Adam nouveau qui mange le vieil homme,
Ta Rome, ton Paris, ta Sparte et ta Sodome,
Comme un pauvre rué parmi d'horribles mets.   4

Mon amour est le feu qui dévore à jamais
Toute chair insensée, et l'évapore comme
Un parfum,—et c'est le déluge qui consomme
En son flot tout mauvais germe que je semais,   8

Afin qu'un jour la Croix où je meurs fût dressée
Et que par un miracle effrayant de bonté
Je t'eusse un jour à moi, frémissant et dompté.

Aime. Sors de ta nuit. Aime. C'est ma pensée   12
De toute éternité, pauvre âme délaissée,
Que tu dusses m'aimer, moi seul qui suis resté!

(vi)

Seigneur, j'ai peur. Mon âme en moi tressaille toute.
Je vois, je sens qu'il faut vous aimer: mais comment
Moi, ceci, me ferai-je, ô vous Dieu, votre amant,
O Justice que la vertu des bons redoute?   4

Oui, comment? car voici que s'ébranle la voûte
Où mon cœur creusait son ensevelissement
Et que je sens fluer à moi le firmament,
Et je vous dis: de vous à moi quelle est la route?   8

Tendez-moi votre main, que je puisse lever
Cette chair accroupie et cet esprit malade!
Mais recevoir jamais la céleste accolade,

Est-ce possible? Un jour, pouvoir la retrouver   12
Dans votre sein, sur votre cœur qui fut le nôtre,
La place où reposa la tête de l'apôtre?

(vii)

Certes, si tu le veux mériter, mon fils, oui,
Et voici. Laisse aller l'ignorance indécise
De ton cœur vers les bras ouverts de mon Église
Comme la guêpe vole au lis épanoui.   4

Approche-toi de mon oreille. Épanches-y
L'humiliation d'une brave franchise.
Dis-moi tout sans un mot d'orgueil ou de reprise
Et m'offre le bouquet d'un repentir choisi.   8

Puis franchement et simplement viens à ma table
Et je t'y bénirai d'un repas délectable
Auquel l'ange n'aura lui-même qu'assisté,

Et tu boiras le vin de la vigne immuable   12
Dont la force, dont la douceur, dont la bonté
Feront germer ton sang à l'immortalité.

Puis, va! Garde une foi modeste en ce mystère
D'amour par quoi je suis ta chair et ta raison,
Et surtout reviens très souvent dans ma maison,
Pour y participer au Vin qui désaltère,   4

Au Pain sans qui la vie est une trahison,
Pour y prier mon Père et supplier ma Mère
Qu'il te soit accordé, dans l'exil de la terre,
D'être l'agneau sans cris qui donne sa toison,   8

D'être l'enfant vêtu de lin et d'innocence,
D'oublier ton pauvre amour-propre et ton essence,
Enfin, de devenir un peu semblable à moi

Qui fus, durant les jours d'Hérode et de Pilate   12
Et de Judas et de Pierre, pareil à toi
Pour souffrir et mourir d'une mort scélérate!

Et pour récompenser ton zele en ces devoirs
Si doux qu'ils sont encor d'ineffables délices,
Je te ferai goûter sur terre mes prémices:
La paix du cœur, l'amour d'être pauvre, et mes soirs   4

Mystiques, quand l'esprit s'ouvre aux calmes espoirs
Et croit boire, suivant ma promesse, au Calice
Éternel, et qu'au ciel pieux la lune glisse,
Et que sonnent les angélus roses et noirs,   8

En attendant l'assomption dans ma lumière,
L'éveil sans fin dans ma charité coutumière,
La musique de mes louanges à jamais,

Et l'extase perpétuelle et la science,   12
Et d'être en moi parmi l'aimable irradiance
De tes souffrances, enfin miennes, que j'aimais!

(viii)

Ah! Seigneur, qu'ai-je? Hélas, me voici tout en larmes
D'une joie extraordinaire: votre voix
Me fait comme du bien et du mal à la fois,
Et le mal et le bien, tout a les mêmes charmes.   4

Je ris, je pleure, et c'est comme un appel aux armes
D'un clairon pour des champs de bataille où je vois
Des anges bleus et blancs portés sur des pavois,
Et ce clairon m'enlève en de fières alarmes.   8

J'ai l'extase et j'ai la terreur d'être choisi.
Je suis indigne, mais je sais votre clémence,
Ah, quel effort, mais quelle ardeur! Et me voici

Plein d'une humble prière, encor qu'un trouble immense 12
Brouille l'espoir que votre voix me révéla,
Et j'aspire en tremblant.

(ix)

—Pauvre âme, c'est cela!

III

i

Désormais le Sage, puni
Pour avoir trop aimé les choses,
Rendu prudent à l'infini,
Mais franc de scrupules moroses,   4

Et d'ailleurs retournant au Dieu
Qui fit les yeux et la lumière,
L'honneur, la gloire, et tout le peu
Qu'a son âme de candeur fière,   8

Le Sage peut, dorénavant,
Assister aux scènes du monde,
Et suivre la chanson du vent,
Et contempler la mer profonde.   12

Il ira, calme, et passera
Dans la férocite des villes,
Comme un mondain à l'Opéra
Qui sort blasé des danses viles.   16

Même, et pour tenir abaissé
L'orgueil, qui fit son âme veuve,
Il remontera le passé,
Ce passé, comme un mauvais fleuve!   20

Il reverra l'herbe des bords,
Il entendra le flot qui pleure
Sur le bonheur mort et les torts
De cette date et de cette heure! . . .   24

Il aimera les cieux, les champs,
La bonté, l'ordre et l'harmonie,
Et sera doux, même aux méchants,
Afin que leur mort soit bénie.   28

Délicat et non exclusif,
Il sera du jour où nous sommes :
Son cœur, plutôt contemplatif,
Pourtant, saura l'œuvre des hommes,   32

Mais revenu des passions,
Un peu méfiant des « usages »,
A vos civilisations
Préférera les paysages.   36

ii

Du fond du grabat
As-tu vu l'étoile
Que l'hiver dévoile ?
Comme ton cœur bat,
Comme cette idée,   5
Regret ou désir,
Ravage à plaisir
Ta tête obsédée
Pauvre tête en feu,
Pauvre cœur sans dieu !   10

L'ortie et l'herbette
Au bas du rempart
D'où l'appel frais part
D'une aigre trompette,
Le vent du coteau,   15
La Meuse, la goutte
Qu'on boit sur la route
A chaque écriteau,
Les sèves qu'on hume,
Les pipes qu'on fume !   20

Un rêve de froid :
« Que c'est beau la neige
Et tout son cortège
Dans leur cadre étroit !
Oh ! tes blancs arcanes,   25

Nouvelle Archangel,
Mirage éternel
De mes caravanes!
Oh! ton chaste ciel,
Nouvelle Archangel!» 30

Cette ville sombre!
Tout est crainte ici . . .
Le ciel est transi
D'éclairer tant d'ombre.
Les pas que tu fais 35
Parmi ces bruyères
Lèvent des poussières
Au souffle mauvais . . .
Voyageur si triste,
Tu suis quelle piste? 40

C'est l'ivresse à mort,
C'est la noire orgie,
C'est l'amer effort
De ton énergie
Vers l'oubli dolent 45
De la voix intime,
C'est le seuil du crime,
C'est l'essor sanglant.
—Oh! fuis la chimère:
Ta mère, ta mère! 50

Quelle est cette voix
Qui ment et qui flatte?
«Ah! Ta tête plate,
Vipère des bois!»
Pardon et mystère. 55
Laisse ça dormir.
Qui peut, sans frémir,
Juger sur la terre?
«Ah! pourtant, pourtant,
Ce monstre impudent!» 60

La mer! Puisse-t-elle
Laver ta rancœur
La mer au grand cœur,
Ton aïeule, celle
Qui chante en berçant   65
Ton angoisse atroce,
La mer, doux colosse
Au sein innocent,
Grondeuse infinie
De ton ironie!   70

Tu vis sans savoir!
Tu verses ton âme,
Ton lait et ta flamme
Dans quel désespoir?
Ton sang aui s'amasse   75
En une fleur d'or
N'est pas prêt encor
A la dédicace.
Attends quelque peu,
Ceci n'est que jeu.   80

Cette frénésie
T'initie au but.
D'ailleurs, le salut
Viendra d'un Messie
Dont tu ne sens plus,   85
Depuis bien des lieues,
Les effluves bleues
Sous tes bras perclus,
Naufragé d'un rêve
Qui n'a pas de grève!   90

Vis en attendant
L'heure toute proche.
Ne sois pas prudent.
Trêve à tout reproche.
Fais ce que tu veux.   95
Une main te guide

A travers le vide
Affreux de tes vœux.
Un peu de courage,
C'est le bon orage.   100

Voici le Malheur
Dans sa plénitude.
Mais à sa main rude
Quelle belle fleur!
«La brûlante épine!»   105
Un lis est moins blanc,
«Elle m'entre au flanc.»
Et l'odeur divine!
«Elle m'entre au cœur.»
Le parfum vainqueur!   110

«Pourtant je regrette,
Pourtant je me meurs,
Pourtant ces deux cœurs . . .»
Lève un peu la tête.
«Eh bien, c'est la Croix.»   115
Lève un peu ton âme
De ce monde infâme.
«Est-ce que je crois?»
Qu'en sais-tu? La Bête
Ignore sa tête,   120

La Chair et le Sang
Méconnaissent l'Acte.
«Mais j'ai fait un pacte
Qui va m'enlaçant
A la faute noire,   125
Je me dois à mon
Tenace démon,
Je ne veux point croire.
Je n'ai pas besoin
De rêver si loin!   130

Aussi bien j'écoute
Des sons d'autrefois.
Vipère des bois,
Encor sur ma route ?
Cette fois, tu mords. »   135
Laisse cette bête.
Que fait au poète ?
Que sont des cœurs morts ?
Ah! plutôt oublie
Ta propre folie.   140

Ah! plutôt, surtout,
Douceur, patience,
Mi-voix et nuance,
Et paix jusqu'au bout !
Aussi bon que sage,   145
Simple autant que bon,
Soumets ta raison
Au plus pauvre adage,
Naïf et discret,
Heureux en secret !   150

Ah! surtout, terrasse
Ton orgueil cruel,
Implore la grâce
D'être un pur Abel,
Finis l'odyssée   155
Dans le repentir
D'un humble martyr,
D'une humble pensée.
Regarde au-dessus . . .
« Est-ce vous, JÉSUS ? »   160

iii

L'espoir luit comme un brin de paille dans l'étable.
Que crains-tu de la guêpe ivre de son vol fou ?
Vois, le soleil toujours poudroie à quelque trou.
Que ne t'endormais-tu, le coude sur la table ?   4

Pauvre âme pâle, au moins cette eau du puits glacé,
Bois-la. Puis dors après. Allons, tu vois, je reste,
Et je dorloterai les rêves de ta sieste,
Et tu chantonneras comme un enfant bercé.   8

Midi sonne. De grâce, éloignez-vous, madame.
Il dort. C'est étonnant comme les pas de femme
Résonnent au cerveau des pauvres malheureux.

Midi sonne. J'ai fait arroser dans la chambre.   12
Va, dors! L'espoir luit comme un caillou dans un creux.
Ah! quand refleuriront les roses de septembre!

iv

Gaspard Hauser chante:
Je suis venu, calme orphelin,
Riche de mes seuls yeux tranquilles,
Vers les hommes des grandes villes:
Ils ne m'ont pas trouvé malin.   4

A vingt ans un trouble nouveau,
Sous le nom d'amoureuses flammes,
M'a fait trouver belles les femmes:
Elles ne m'ont pas trouvé beau.   8

Bien que sans patrie et sans roi
Et très brave ne l'étant guère,
J'ai voulu mourir à la guerre:
La mort n'a pas voulu de moi.   12

Suis-je né trop tôt ou trop tard?
Qu'est-ce que je fais en ce monde?
O vous tous, ma peine est profonde:
Priez pour le pauvre Gaspard!   16

v

Un grand sommeil noir
Tombe sur ma vie:
Dormez, tout espoir,
Dormez, toute envie!   4

Je ne vois plus rien,
Je perds la mémoire
Du mal et du bien . . .
O la triste histoire!   8

Je suis un berceau
Qu'une main balance
Au creux d'un caveau:
Silence, silence!   1 2

vi

Le ciel est, par-dessus le toit,
    Si bleu, si calme!
Un arbre, par-dessus le toit,
    Berce sa palme.   4

La cloche, dans le ciel qu'on voit,
    Doucement tinte.
Un oiseau sur l'arbre qu'on voit
    Chante sa plainte.   8

Mon Dieu, mon Dieu, la vie est là,
    Simple et tranquille.
Cette paisible rumeur-là
    Vient de la ville.   1 2

—Qu'as-tu fait, ô toi que voilà
    Pleurant sans cesse,
Dis, qu'as-tu fait, toi que voilà,
    De ta jeunesse?   1 6

vii

Je ne sais pourquoi
Mon esprit amer
D'une aile inquiète et folle vole sur la mer.   3
Tout ce qui m'est cher,
D'une aile d'effroi
Mon amour le couve au ras des flots. Pourquoi, pourquoi ?   6

Mouette à l'essor mélancolique,
Elle suit la vague, ma pensée,
A tous les vents du ciel balancée   9
Et biaisant quand la marée oblique,
Mouette à l'essor mélancolique.

Ivre de soleil   12
Et de liberté,
Un instinct la guide à travers cette immensité.
La brise d'été   15
Sur le flot vermeil
Doucement la porte en un tiède demi-sommeil.

Parfois si tristement elle crie   18
Qu'elle alarme au lointain le pilote,
Puis au gré du vent se livre et flotte
Et plonge, et l'aile toute meurtrie   21
Revole, et puis si tristement crie !

Je ne sais pourquoi
Mon esprit amer   24
D'une aile inquiète et folle vole sur la mer.
Tout ce qui m'est cher,
D'une aile d'effroi   27
Mon amour le couve au ras des flots. Pourquoi, pourquoi ?

viii

Parfums, couleurs, systèmes, lois!
Les mots ont peur comme des poules.
La chair sanglote sur la croix.   3

Pied, c'est du rêve que tu foules,
Et partout ricane la voix,
La voix tentatrice des foules.   6

Cieux bruns où nagent nos desseins,
Fleurs qui n'êtes pas le calice,
Vin et ton geste qui se glisse,   9
Femme et l'œillade de tes seins,

Nuit câline aux frais traversins,
Qu'est-ce que c'est que ce délice,   12
Qu'est-ce que c'est que ce supplice,
Nous les damnés et vous les Saints?

ix

Le son du cor s'afflige vers les bois
D'une douleur on veut croire orpheline
Qui vient mourir au bas de la colline
Parmi la bise errant en courts abois.   4

L'âme du loup pleure dans cette voix
Qui monte avec le soleil qui décline
D'une agonie on veut croire câline
Et qui ravit et qui navre à la fois.   8

Pour faire mieux cette plainte assoupie,
La neige tombe à longs traits de charpie
A travers le couchant sanguinolent,

Et l'air a l'air d'être un soupir d'automne,   12
Tant il fait doux par ce soir monotone
Où se dorlote un paysage lent.

x

La tristesse, la langueur du corps humain
M'attendrissent, me fléchissent, m'apitoient.
Ah! surtout quand des sommeils noirs le foudroient,
Quand les draps zèbrent la peau, foulent la main!   4

Et que mièvre dans la fièvre du demain,
Tiède encor du bain de sueur qui décroît,
Comme un oiseau qui grelotte sur un toit!
Et les pieds, toujours douloureux du chemin,   8

Et les sein, marqué d'un double coup de poing,
Et la bouche, une blessure rouge encor,
Et la chair frémissante, frêle décor,

Et les yeux, les pauvres yeux si beaux où point   12
La douleur de voir encore du fini! . . .
Triste corps! Combien faible et combien puni!

xi

La bise se rue à travers
Les buissons tout noirs et tout verts,
Glaçant la neige éparpillée
Dans la campagne ensoleillée.   4
L'odeur est aigre près des bois,
L'horizon chante avec des voix,
Les coqs des clochers des villages
Luisent crûment sur les nuages.   8
C'est délicieux de marcher
A travers ce brouillard léger

Qu'un vent taquin parfois retrousse.
Ah! fi de mon vieux feu qui tousse! 12
J'ai des fourmis plein les talons.
Debout, mon âme, vite, allons!
C'est le printemps sévère encore,
Mais qui par instant s'édulcore 16
D'un souffle tiède juste assez
Pour mieux sentir les froids passés
Et penser au Dieu de clémence . . .
Va, mon âme, à l'espoir immense! 20

xii

Vous voilà, vous voilà, pauvres bonnes pensées!
L'espoir qu'il faut, regret des grâces dépensées,
Douceur de cœur avec sévérité d'esprit,
Et cette vigilance, et le calme prescrit, 4
Et toutes!—Mais encor lentes, bien éveillées,
Bien d'aplomb, mais encor timides, débrouillées
A peine du lourd rêve et de la tiède nuit.
C'est à qui de vous va plus gauche; l'une suit 8
L'autre, et toutes ont peur du vaste clair de lune.
«Telles, quand les brebis sortent d'un clos. C'est une,
Puis deux, puis trois. Le reste est là, les yeux baissés,
La tête à terre, et l'air des plus embarrassés, 12
Faisant ce que fait leur chef de file: il s'arrête,
Elles s'arrêtent tour à tour, posant leur tête
Sur son dos, simplement et sans savoir pourquoi.»[1]
Votre pasteur, ô mes brebis, ce n'est pas moi, 16
C'est un meilleur, un bien meilleur, qui sait les causes,
Lui qui vous tint longtemps et si longtemps là closes,
Mais qui vous délivra de sa main au temps vrai.
Suivez-le. Sa houlette est bonne. 20
                         Et je serai,
Sous sa voix toujours douce à votre ennui qui bêle,
Je serai, moi, par nos chemins, son chien fidèle.

[1] Dante: *Le Purgatoire*

xiii

L'échelonnement des haies
Moutonne à l'infini, mer
Claire dans le brouillard clair
Qui sent bon les jeunes baies.   4

Des arbres et des moulins
Sont légers sur le vert tendre
Où vient s'ébattre et s'étendre
L'agilité des poulains.   8

Dans ce vague d'un Dimanche
Voici se jouer aussi
De grandes brebis aussi
Douces que leur laine blanche.   12

Tout à l'heure déferlait
L'onde, roulée en volutes,
De cloches comme des flûtes
Dans le ciel comme du lait.   16

xiv

L'immensité de l'humanité,
Le Temps passé, vivace et bon père,
Une entreprise à jamais prospère:
Quelle puissante et calme cité!   4

Il semble ici qu'on vit dans l'histoire.
Tout est plus fort que l'homme d'un jour.
De lourds rideaux d'atmosphère noire
Font richement la nuit alentour.   8

O civilisés que civilise
L'Ordre obéi, le Respect sacré!
O dans ce champ si bien préparé
Cette moisson de la Seule Église!   12

XV

La mer est plus belle
Que les cathédrales,
Nourrice fidèle,   3
Berceuse de râles,
La mer sur qui prie
La Vierge Marie!   6

Elle a tous les dons
Terribles et doux.
J'entends ses pardons   9
Gronder ses courroux . . .
Cette immensité
N'a rien d'entêté.   12

Oh! si patiente,
Même quand méchante!
Un souffle ami hante   15
La vague, et nous chante:
«Vous sans espérance,
Mourez sans souffrance!»   18

Et puis sous les cieux
Qui s'y rient plus clairs,
Elle a des airs bleus,   21
Roses, gris et verts . . .
Plus belle que tous,
Meilleure que nous!   24

xvi

La «grande ville»! Un tas criard de pierres blanches
Où rage le soleil comme en pays conquis.
Tous les vices ont leur tanière, les exquis
Et les hideux, dans ce désert de pierres blanches.   4

Des odeurs! Des bruits vains! Où que vague le cœur,
Toujours ce poudroiement vertigineux de sable,
Toujours ce remuement de la chose coupable
Dans cette solitude où s'écœure le cœure! 8

De près, de loin, le Sage aura sa Thébaïde
Parmi le fade ennui qui monte de ceci,
D'autant plus âpre et plus sanctifiante aussi
Que deux parts de son âme y pleurent, dans ce vide! 12

xvii

Tournez, tournez, bons chevaux de bois,
Tournez cent tours, tournez mille tours,
Tournez souvent et tournez toujours,
Tournez, tournez au son des hautbois. 4

L'enfant tout rouge et la mère blanche,
Le gars en noir et la fille en rose,
L'une à la chose et l'autre à la pose,
Chacun se paie un sou de dimanche. 8

Tournez, tournez, chevaux de leur cœur,
Tandis qu'autour de tous vos tournois
Clignote l'œil du filou sournois
Tournez au son du piston vainqueur! 12

C'est étonnant comme ça vous soûle
D'aller ainsi dans ce cirque bête:
Bien dans le ventre et mal dans la tête,
Du mal en masse et du bien en foule. 16

Tournez au son de l'accordéon,
Du violon, du trombone fous,
Chevaux plus doux que des moutons, doux
Comme un peuple en révolution. 20

Le vent, fouettant la tente, les verres,
Les zincs et le drapeau tricolore,
Et les jupons, et que sais-je encore?
Fait un fracas de cinq cents tonnerres.   24

Tournez, dadas, sans qu'il soit besoin
D'user jamais de nuls éperons
Pour commander à vos galops ronds:
Tournez, tournez, sans espoir de foin.   28

Et dépêchez, chevaux de leur âme:
Déjà voici que sonne à la soupe
La nuit qui tombe et chasse la troupe
Des gais buveurs que leur soif affame.   32

Tournez, tournez! Le ciel en velours
D'astres en or se vêt lentement.
L'église tinte un glas tristement.
Tournez au son joyeux des tambours!   36

xviii

Parisien, mon frère à jamais étonné,
Montons sur la colline où le soleil est né
Si glorieux qu'il fait comprendre l'idolâtre,
Sous cette perspective, inconnue au théâtre,   4
D'arbres au vent et de poussière d'ombre et d'or.
Montons. Il fait si frais encor, montons encor.
Là! nous voilà «placés» comme dans une «loge
De face», et le «décor» vraiment tire un éloge.   8
La cathédrale énorme et le beffroi sans fin,
Ces toits de tuile sous ces verdures, le vain
Appareil des remparts pompeux et grands quand même.
Ces clochers, cette tour, ces autres, sur l'or blême   12
Des nuages à l'ouest réverbérant l'or dur
De derrière *chez nous*, tous ces lourds joyaux sur
Ces ouates, n'est-ce pas, l'écrin vaut le voyage,

Et c'est ce qu'on peut dire un brin de paysage?   16
—Mais descendons, si ce n'est trop abuser
De vos pieds las, à fin seule de reposer
Vos yeux qui n'ont jamais rien vu que de Montmartre,
—«Campagne» vert de plaie, et ville blanc de dartre   20
(Et les sombres parfums qui grimpent de Pantin!)—
Donc, par ce lent sentier de rosée et de thym,
Cheminons vers la ville au long de la rivière,
Sous les frais peupliers, dans la fine lumière.   24
L'une des portes ouvre une rue, entrons-y.
Aussi bien, c'est le point qu'il faut, l'endroit choisi:
Si blanches, les maisons anciennes, si bien faites,
Point hautes, çà et là des branches sur leurs faîtes,   28
Si doux et sinueux le cours de ces maisons,
Comme un ruisseau parmi de vagues frondaisons,
Profilant la lumière et l'ombre en broderies
Au lieu du long ennui de vos haussmanneries,   32
Et si gentil l'accent qui confine au patois
De ces passants naïfs avec leurs yeux matois!...
Des places ivres d'air et de cris d'hirondelles,
Où l'Histoire proteste en formules fidèles   36
A la crête des toits comme au fer des balcons,
Des portes ne tournant qu'à regret sur leurs gonds,
Jalouses de garder l'honneur et la famille...
Ici tout vit et meurt calme, rien ne fourmille,   40
Le «Théâtre» *fait four*, et ce dieu des brouillons,
Le «Journal» n'en est plus à compter ses *bouillons*,
L'amour même prétend conserver ses noblesses,
Et le vice *se gobe* en de rares drôlesses.   44
Enfin, rien de Paris, mon frère, «dans nos murs».
Que les modes... d'hier, et que les fruits bien mûrs
De ce fameux progrès que vous mangez en herbe.
Du reste on vit à l'aise. Une chère superbe,   48
La raison raisonnable et l'esprit des aïeux,
Beaucoup de sain travail, quelques loisirs joyeux,
Et ce besoin d'avoir peur de la grande route!...
Avouvez, la province est bonne, somme toute,   52
Et vous regrettez moins que tantôt la «splendeur»
Du vieux monstre, et son pouls fébrile, et cette odeur!

xix

C'est la fête du blé, c'est la fête du pain
Aux chers lieux d'autrefois revus après ces choses!
Tout bruit, la nature et l'homme, dans un bain
De lumière si blanc que les ombres sont roses.　　4

L'or des pailles s'effondre au vol siffleur des faux
Dont l'éclair plonge, et va luire, et se réverbère.
La plaine, tout au loin couverte de travaux,
Change de face à chaque instant, gaie et sévère.　　8

Tout halète, tout n'est qu'effort et mouvement
Sous le soleil, tranquille auteur des moissons mûres,
Et qui travaille encore, imperturbablement,
A gonfler, à sucrer là-bas les grappes sures.　　12

Travaille, vieux soleil, pour le pain et le vin,
Nourris l'homme du lait de la terre, et lui donne
L'honnête verre où rit un peu d'oubli divin.
Moissonneurs, vendangeurs là-bas, votre heure est bonne!　16

Car sur la fleur des pains et sur la fleur des vins,
Fruit de la force humaine en tous lieux répartie,
Dieu moissonne, et vendange, et dispose à ses fins
La Chair et le Sang pour le calice et l'hostie!　　20

FIN

COMMENTARIES

DEDICATION

The dedication was altered in the second edition of 1889 to: 'A la mémoire de ma mère', Mme. Verlaine having died on 21 January 1886. The relationship between Mme. Verlaine and her only child had always been an extremely close one—and during the years of *Sagesse* in particular the poet had found in his mother an unfailing source of comfort and consolation.

PREFACE

In the second edition Verlaine retained the preface but headed it: 'Préface de la première edition', thus implicitly admitting that the pious and penitent note of these lines was quite out of keeping with the way of life into which he had fallen by 1889. Ernest Delahaye makes this point in his 'avertissement' to the facsimile edition of the manuscript of the 1881 edition which Verlaine gave him (see E. Delahaye, *Sagesse, Les Manuscrits des Maîtres*, Messein, 1913).

I

i. *Bon chevalier masqué . . .*

According to the annotated copy this poem was 'écrit à Stickney (Lincolnshire, Angleterre) en été 1875, sur l'herbe d'une prairie où paissaient des vaches'. The date is no doubt correct, but the poem looks back of course to the previous year in prison and is an allegory of the arrival of the unhappy news that Mathilde had obtained a legal separation, which turned out to have a paradoxically good effect in that it was due to this 'bon chevalier Malheur' that Verlaine's thoughts turned in a religious direction. In *Mes Prisons* (chapter 12) Verlaine recalls this episode in a much more prosaic manner: 'Jésus, comme vous vous y prîtes vous pour me prendre! Ah!—un matin, le bon Directeur lui-même entra dans ma cellule:—Mon pauvre ami, me dit-il, je vous apporte un mauvais message. Du courage. Lisez!' (*Œuvres complètes*, ii, p. 769). The typically Verlainian conversational expression that ends the poem (It's alright this time', or 'Don't let it happen again') is repeated at the end of 'Le dernier dizain' in *Parallèlement*, again in reference to the period of imprisonment in Belgium.

V. P. Underwood (*Verlaine et l'Angleterre*, p. 238) perceives in the medieval atmosphere of the poem the influence of the Arthurian *Idylls* of Tennyson, whom Verlaine mentions in a letter from Stickney to Emile Blémont dated 19 November 1875. The same critic further suggests (op. cit., p. 241) that line 9 may have been inspired by two lines from Marlowe's *Dr. Faustus*:

> Oh, I grow dull, the cold hand of sleep
> Hath thrust icy fingers in my breast.

ii. *J'avais peiné comme Sisyphe* . . .

'Fait à Arras (Pas-de-Calais) un après-midi, chez ma mère, vers Septembre 1875', according to the annotated copy. This is therefore one of the first of several poems in which Verlaine describes his struggle against the temptations of the flesh.

Like *Bon chevalier masqué* . . . the poem is in the form of an allegory and has a similiar medieval and Tennysonian flavour, despite the opening classical references, firstly to Sisyphus's endless struggle to roll a boulder up a mountain only to see it roll down again, secondly to the twelve labours of Hercules, thirdly to the prowess in battle of Achilles and lastly, in stanza seven, to one of the Gorgons, the three female monsters of Greek mythology.

The *terza rima* pattern in which the poem is written is the one used in *The Divine Comedy*, which Verlaine mentions in a letter to Ernest Delahaye on 1 July 1875, and the way in which the figure of prayer appears to the poet is reminiscent of the way Virgil appears to Dante at the beginning of the latter's poem. Bunyan's *Pilgrim's Progress* to which Verlaine refers in letters to Emile Blémont and Ernest Delahaye may also, according to V. P. Underwood (op. cit., pp. 245–8), have influenced this poem in that the personification of the flesh as an 'âpre géante' is reminiscent of Bunyan's personification of Despair as a giant. The same critic further suggests (op. cit., p. 225) that there may be some influence of the hymns which Verlaine heard and appreciated as a regular churchgoer during his stay in Lincolnshire. Lines 59–61 in particular could echo a well-known hymn which urges the faithful to 'watch and pray', but since the 'Quelqu'un' is Christ they may well echo instead the lines from Mark xiv. 38 where Christ counsels his disciples: 'Watch and pray lest ye enter into temptation', as L. Morice points out in his edition of *Sagesse*. V. P. Underwood finally suggests, (op. cit., 235) that the use of allegory and the pastoral setting of this and the preceding poem may be due in some measure to Milton's masque *Comus* to which Verlaine refers in a letter dated 7 May 1875. In stanza three the 'farouche ami qui m'accompagnes' is one half of Verlaine's personality, his 'courage païen' by which he means human courage as distinct from the divine courage which prayer gives him.

iii. *Qu'en dis-tu, voyageur . . .*

'Fait à Arras, chez ma mère, septembre-octobre 1875', according to the annotated copy, Verlaine having forgotten that he had resumed his duties at Stickney on 13 September 1875. Behind the figure representing 'la sagesse humaine' who speaks for the first thirteen stanzas, it is generally agreed that Arthur Rimbaud can be perceived. The note of mockery and sarcasm in these stanzas is very characteristic of the attitude of 'l'époux infernal' towards the 'vierge folle' in Rimbaud's *Une Saison en Enfer*. But although the poem refers to the vagabond life Verlaine and Rimbaud led from July 1872 until July 1873, it also echoes, in the way it lays bare a sense of disillusion, Baudelaire's *Le Voyage*:

> Etonnants voyageurs . . .
> Dites, qu'avez-vous vu . . .

V. P. Underwood suggests (op. cit., p. 241) that lines 41–4 may owe something to Tennyson's description of the sword Excalibur in *Morte d'Arthur*:

> the great brand
> Made lightnings in the splendour of the moon
> And flashing round and round and whirl'd in an arch
> Shot like a streamer of the northern morn.

Line 16 provides the first of several examples in *Sagesse* of the cæsura after the sixth syllable in an alexandrine being completely suppressed. In the last line of the poem too the word 'méchanceté' covers the fifth, sixth, seventh and eighth syllables so that even the slightest pause after the sixth syllable is impossible. Rimbaud had drawn attention to Verlaine's boldness in this respect as early as *Fêtes galantes* when he wrote that there were 'parfois de fortes licences: ainsi "Et la tigresse épou-vantable d'Hyrcanie' est un vers de ce volume"' (letter to Izambard 25 August 1870, *Rimbaud, Œuvres complètes*, Bibliothèque de la Pléiade, 1963, p. 259).

iv. *Malheureux, tous les dons . . .*

The annotated copy gives the same date as for the previous poem and again therefore the date must be corrected to early September 1875. Verlaine also notes that the poem was written 'à propos d'Arthur Rimbaud', so that if it is Rimbaud who is lecturing and even hectoring Verlaine in the previous poem (and receiving a soft answer in the last four stanzas) the rôles are reversed in this lengthy diatribe. It must be said however that in the annotated copy Verlaine added: 'Après coup, je me suis aperçu que cela pouvait s'appliquer a "poor myself" '. V. P. Underwood notes (op. cit., pp. 234–5) that the seventeenth-century poet George Herbert, in his poem *Miserie*, roundly castigates a sinner who is revealed, in the last line of the poem, to be himself.

v. *Beauté des femmes . . .*

'Arras, septembre ou octobre 1875. Après quelle tentation!', states the annotated copy, but, as with the two preceding poems this sonnet must have been written in early September and was in fact sent to Emile Blémont in a letter from Stickney dated 20 September. This is one of the poems Verlaine asked Blémont to submit to the editors of the third volume of *Le Parnasse contemporain* but all were rejected by Anatole France with the comment: 'Non. L'auteur est indigne, et les vers sont des plus mauvais qu'on ait vus'. Technically the poem is interesting in that the quatrains give the impression of containing false rhymes, that is masculine rhymes accompanying feminine rhymes, although in fact the first line of each quatrain rhymes not with the second line but with the fourth. All the rhymes in the quatrains are based on the vowel 'a' as are all the rhymes in the tercets except the last, and as well as this extensive assonance Verlaine also makes an effective use of alliteration in the fifth and sixth lines, where the repeated 'm' sounds have a hypnotic effect, in contrast with the sharp 'k' sounds in the questions put in the last two lines.

V. P. Underwood suggests (op. cit., p. 233) that the exclamatory style of the poem may possibly have been borrowed from the work of George Herbert and notably from his sonnet *Prayer*. The image of the mountain in line 10 is a fairly usual one to describe standing aloof from everyday life and it occurs frequently in the Bible, as, for example, in Luke ix. 28: 'Jesus went up into the mountain to pray'.

vi. *O vous comme un qui boite au loin . . .*

This sonnet was sent to Ernest Delahaye in a letter from Boston dated 23 May 1876, so that the comment on the annotated copy: 'Stickney, été 1875, en revenant d'avoir communié à l'église catholique de Boston' is probably inaccurate as regards the year.

The poem expresses a moment of extreme religious fervour when the old Verlaine, subject to all the vagaries of existence—joys and sorrows, pleasures sought for and pleasures taken (line 4), happiness and unhappiness, laughter and sadness—is banished and replaced by a new Verlaine with a sense of detachment from all these things and a readiness to welcome life calmly as a mere prelude to eternal life. The eighth line is based on the familiar expression: 'broyer du noir', to be down in the dumps.

According to V. P. Underwood (op. cit., p. 247) there may be some influence of Bunyan's *Pilgrim's Progress* in the personification of Sadness in line 8.

vii. *Les faux beaux jours* . . .

'Paris, octobre 1875 (sur le bord d'une rechute)' according to the annotated copy which once more is manifestly inaccurate since in October 1875 Verlaine was not in Paris, nor even in France, as has been mentioned above. Like I v this sonnet was probably written in early September and although Verlaine no doubt paid a visit to Paris at that time (see note to I ix on this page) the second quatrain suggests a country setting. It is just possible that Verlaine could have met Rimbaud again, if the latter returned to Charleville from a trip to Italy earlier than is generally thought and this would certainly explain the sense of extreme anguish which Verlaine is clearly suffering in this sonnet and which is admirably conveyed in the symbolism of the quatrains. This play on the literal and the figurative sense of the word 'day' seems so obvious that it is doubtful if there is any need to see in it, as V. P. Underwood does in *Verlaine et l'Angleterre*, p. 242, yet another example of the influence of Tennyson who in *Guinevere* writes of the guilty Queen Guinevere dreaming that she stood:

> On some vast plain before a setting sun
> And from the sun there swiftly made at her
> A ghastly something . . .

viii. *La vie humble*

'Paris, octobre 1875, après une sévère confession', states the annotated copy which, as with the preceding poem, must be discounted as regards the month of composition of this sonnet which was no doubt written in early September, possibly as a sequel to *Les faux beaux jours* . . .

V. P. Underwood suggests (op. cit., p. 226) that Verlaine may have had in mind here the well-known Anglican hymn: 'The daily round, the common task, should furnish all we ought to ask . . .' and other hymns on a similar theme.

ix. *Sagesse d'un Louis Racine* . . .

'Lors d'un voyage à Versailles, octobre 1875', according to the annotated copy which must again be corrected as regards the month of composition. There is however every reason to accept not only the year but also the place of composition, with Louis XIV's palace inspiring in Verlaine a dream of living in the closing years of the seventeenth century—rather too rosy a dream perhaps, in that France was probably a good deal less happy during the last part of the reign of the 'Roi Soleil', alluded to in line 4, and a good deal less delighted with Madame de Maintenon's excessive piety, alluded to in line 6, than Verlaine supposes. Louis Racine (1692–1763) was the son of the dramatist and wrote religious poems, including a translation of Milton's *Paradise Lost* with which Verlaine was no doubt familiar. Rollin (1661–1741) was a Rector of the University of Paris. The mention of 'poète et docteur' in line 9 may well be an allusion to Jean Racine and his Jansenist friends at Port-Royal. In the final line Garo is a character in the fable 'Le gland et la citrouille' by La Fontaine who shared with other writers of the seventeenth century a liking for the woods of Auteuil west of Paris. With regard to line 1 Jacques Robichez (*Verlaine, Œuvres poétiques*, p. 603) notes that this is the third time the word 'sagesse' which forms the title of the volume has appeared in the poems (c.f. 'J'avais peiné comme Sisyphe . . .' line 65 and 'Malheureux, tous les dons . . .' line 53).

x. *Non, il fut gallican, ce siècle . . .*

'Paris, le lendemain', according to the annotated copy. This sonnet is clearly a reply to the preceding one and it is easy to understand that, on reflection, Verlaine should have realised that his emotional, un-intellectual kind of faith was closer to the fervour of the Middle Ages than to the subtleties of seventeenth-century Jansenism and Gallicanism. At first sight line 3 seems to be an example of Verlaine's liking for familiar expressions, but in view of its context he may well have had in mind the technical sense of 'en panne' which is a nautical term meaning 'hove to'. In line 13 the word 'folie' may seem a strange word to us, but according to Louis Morice it is frequently used in this context in the language of mysticism. It should be noted that in the fourth poem of the sonnet sequence beginning 'Mon Dieu m'a dit . . .' in the second section of *Sagesse* Verlaine uses a similar kind of expression and, in the manuscript version, quotes St. Augustine's phrase: 'Dieu nous a aimés jusqu'à la folie' (see below p. 87). With regard to the rose-coloured spectacles through which Verlaine looks at both the seventeenth century and the Middle Ages in these two sonnets Jacques Robichez rightly comments that 'ces nostalgies sont de nature à faire suspecter non pas sa sincérité (tout laisse croire qu'il les éprouve en effet), mais la profondeur de sa foi' (*Verlaine, Œuvres poétiques*, p. 604).

xi. *Petits amis qui sûtes nous prouver . . .*

Undated in the annotated copy but probably written in 1875 and certainly before the companion piece immediately following. The 'petits amis' are the rationalists whom Verlaine bitterly attacks, countering their arguments with his own simple faith in divine revelation. In line

14 the expression 'logique rance' is meant ironically—a logic judged rancid or out of date by the rationalists. In lines 23 and 24 the elliptic expression: 'c'est nos cercueils, naïfs ou non', means: 'nos cercueils nous attendent, que nous soyons naïfs ou non'; in other words, death awaits us all.

xii. *Or, vous voici promus, petits amis . . .*

Verlaine's religious conversion had been accompanied by a political conversion to Royalism and a violent rejection of his former Republican opinions. In this poem he sees Republicanism as the political face of the philosophy of rationalism on which he has poured scorn in the preceding poem. The date given in the annotated copy: 'Paris, octobre 1875', could well be approximately correct for *Petits amis qui sûtes nous prouver . . .* (always bearing in mind that, as mentioned in the note to I iii, Verlaine had in fact left Paris for England by mid-September 1875), but it is probably incorrect for this one which was obviously written just after a political election, possibly that of January 1879, although the earlier elections of October 1877 and February 1876 were equally disastrous for the royalists and victorious for the Republicans. Line 34 is a Biblical allusion to the incident in the Book of Daniel where Nebuchadnezzar is punished for his pride. In the final lines Verlaine visualises the restoration of the monarchy, symbolised by the white flag of the royalists with its *fleur de lys* emblem waving over the Bastille, the latter being elliptically described as 'absurde' no doubt because of the inordinate importance which, in Verlaine's view, his compatriots attributed to its fall. Teniers, referred to in the next to last line, was a seventeenth-century Belgian painter in vogue in nineteenth-century France whom Verlaine imagines painting the Republicans and Rationalists returning, forgiven, to the bosom of the Church. Line 9 has one syllable too many and so as to correct this mistake Verlaine reversed the order of two words in the 1889 edition where the line reads:

'A l'œuvre, amis petits! Nous avons droit . . .'

xiii. *Prince mort en soldat . . .*

Despite Verlaine's Royalist convictions, he was prepared to accept Bonapartism rather than Republicanism, as is implied in the final stanza of this poem. After the fall of the Second Empire in 1870 Napoleon III lived in England until his death in 1873. His son was killed a few years later on 1 June 1879, not however 'à cause de la France', as Verlaine states, but while serving with the British army in Zululand. Since this news did not reach France for some three weeks, the date given in the annotated copy: 'A propos de la mort du Prince

Impérial, Rethel (Ardennes) où j'étais professeur, le 2 juin de cette année-là', cannot be quite accurate.

xiv. *Vous reviendrez bientôt . . .*

'A propos de l'expulsion des Jésuites. Au lendemain du jour', states the annotated copy, which means that the poem was written on 1 July 1880 since the Jesuits, as a consequence of laws enacted against them by the Republican government, were evicted from their house in the Rue de Sèvres on 30 June 1880. In the 1889 edition line 6 was altered to read: 'Avec la Fleur chérie', which is the 'lys de Louis Seize' of the preceding poem.

xv. *On n'offense que Dieu . . .*

'Pour ma femme séparée, depuis divorcée. Rethel, 1879', according to the annotated copy. But the date is probably wrong and it seems likely that the poem was written shortly after Easter 1878, as were the next three poems. The word 'frère' in line 2 is used in the wide Biblical sense and refers here to Mathilde.

xvi. *Ecoutez la chanson bien douce . . .*

'Pour la même. Même année', according to the annotated copy, but this must mean 1878 rather than 1879 in view of the fact that Verlaine sent a version of this poem to his brother-in-law, Charles de Sivry, in a letter dated 27 October 1878 in which he described it, with a quite unnecessary modesty, as 'cette musicaillerie, sans talent aucun, je le crains'. The use of exclusively feminine rhymes should be noted as contributing greatly to the gentle, cajoling note of the lines. The expressions 'en peine' and 'de passage', presumably because they are familiar to the point of being *clichés*—'une âme en peine', 'la vie n'est qu'un passage'—are italicised in the first edition though not in later editions.

xvii. *Les chères mains . . .*

'Même femme et même date', according to the annotated copy. One might add 'même style' since this poem too is in exclusively feminine rhymes. Lines 3–6 refer to Verlaine's wanderings with Rimbaud, and line 11 to the rumours about the nature of their relationship. The 'complicité maternelle' of line 15 refers to Verlaine's apparently friendly reception by his mother-in-law, Mme. Mauté, when he opened negotiations with her at Easter 1878 about the possibility of making a fresh start with Mathilde (see ex-Mme. Paul Verlaine, *Mémoires de ma vie*, Flammarion, 1935, p. 239).

xviii. *Et j'ai revu l'enfant unique* . . .

'Paris, juin 1881, au sortir d'une entrevue avec mon petit Georges', according to the annotated copy, but the date is patently inaccurate since *Sagesse* had already been published some months before. It was in fact, during the Easter holidays 1878 that Verlaine was allowed to visit his six-year-old son who had been ill and it seems probable that all four of these 'family' poems were written at that time.

xix. *Voix de l'Orgueil* . . .

'Stickney, été 1875, à travers champs'. These details from the annotated copy are probably accurate since Verlaine's confidence in his ability to resist temptation, which he displays so powerfully in this poem, was at its strongest in the first year after his conversion. V. P. Underwood suggests, in *Verlaine et l'Angleterre*, p. 242, that the poem may owe something to Tennyson's *The two voices* and more particularly to the lines:

> From out my sullen heart a power
> Broke, like the rainbow from the shower,
> To feel, although no tongue can prove,
> That every cloud that spreads above
> And veileth love itself is love.

From the technical point of view it has been suggested that Verlaine may have been influenced by Baudelaire's *Les Phares* and by Rimbaud's *Les Voyelles* in the first four quatrains where he evokes the various temptations in a series of telling images, instead of trying to describe and define them. The unusual rhyme scheme should be noted and has been mentioned above in the introduction, p. 12.

xx. *L'ennemi se déguise en l'ennui* . . .

'Paris, 1879' is the laconic comment in the annotated copy, but the use of 'vers impairs' and Verlaine's continuing struggle against temptation could suggest a considerably earlier date and the appeal for divine help in the struggle against the devil, who can deprive him of the will to resist, is reminiscent of the theme of I ii, written in 1875.

xxi. *Va ton chemin* . . .

'Paris, 1880', according to the annotated copy, but the unusual rhyme scheme, with false rhymes between the final lines of each stanza, and the mood of calm assurance suggest a considerably earlier date. The poem is reminiscent of Bunyan's *Pilgrim's Progress* which, as has already been mentioned, Verlaine was reading in November 1875.

xxii. *Pourquoi triste, ô mon âme . . .*

Again 'Paris, 1880', according to the annotated copy, but as well as the
Biblical inspiration of the opening lines (see Ps. 42: 5, and Matt. 26: 38)
there may be echoes of *Pilgrim's Progress* and this fact, plus the general
theme of the poem would suggest a date nearer to 1875.

xxiii. *Né l'enfant des grandes villes . . .*

'Paris, 1880. Cette prière et le précédentes écrites après bien des luttes,
victorieuses encore', (annotated copy). But by 1880 the period of
Verlaine's 'luttes victorieuses' was virtually over and the liaison with
Lucien Létinois had begun. Once again therefore a much earlier date
for the poem seems likely and once again the rhyme scheme, with
false rhymes between the final lines of each stanza, as in *Va ton
chemin . . .*, lends support to this suggestion, along with the fact that the
poem is in 'vers impairs' and that there are renewed echoes of *Pilgrim's
Progress*.

xxiv. *L'âme antique . . .*

'Arras, automne 1875', according to the annotated copy. It is not often that
Verlaine's poems have as markedly intellectual a content as this study of
maternal sorrow, of which Hecuba, queen of Troy, and Niobé, queen of
Phrygia, who both lost all their sons, are classical examples, and with
whom Verlaine contrasts, in the last half of the poem, the supreme
Christian example of maternal sorrow, the Virgin Mary. Lines 9-16
allude to the legend of Hecuba flinging herself into the Hellespont and
being metamorphosed into a dog. Line 40 is an allusion to one of the titles of
the Virgin Mary, Our Lady of Dolours, whose feast day falls on 15
September, which could conceivably therefore be the precise date of the
poem, although in that case the place of composition would need to be
corrected in view of Verlaine's return to Stickney on 13 September
1875.

II

i. *O mon Dieu vous m'avez blessé d'amour . . .*

This poem, in the form of a litany, unrhymed, save for the last line, was
dated 'juillet 1875' when it was sent to Blémont in a letter dated from
19 November of that year. The annotated copy is therefore at fault in
dating the poem: 'Mons, Belgique, de la prison, 1874, 15 août'. Louis
Morice however suggests, in his edition of *Sagesse*, that 'lieu et date ne
sont faux que matériellement' (p. 261), adding that no poem could have
brought back to Verlaine better than this one what he himself called

'l'immense sensation de fraîcheur, de renoncement, de résignation éprouvée en cette inoubliable jour de l'Assomption 1874' (*Mes Prisons, Œuvres complètes*, ii, p. 776).

V. P. Underwood (op. cit., p. 227) sees, in the last line of the poem, an echo of a line from an Anglican hymn: 'All that I have or am is thine', and suggests that there are also echoes of other hymns elsewhere in the poem. The same critic notes (op. cit., p. 234) a certain resemblance between stanzas 8, 10 and 11 and the following lines from George Herbert's *The Convert*:

> If ever tears did flow from eyes,
> If ever voice was hoarse with cries,
> If ever heart was sore with sighs,
> Let now my eyes, my voice, my heart
> Strive each to play their part.

ii. *Je ne veux plus aimer que ma mère Marie . . .*

This poem too was sent to Blémont in the letter of 19 November 1875, where it is dated 'août 1875' although the annotated copy gives it the same date and place of composition as the preceding poem. It is the only poem in *Sagesse* addressed to the Virgin Mary, surprisingly perhaps in view of Verlaine's fervent catholicism and his compulsive desire for protection and consolation.

iii. *Vous êtes calme . . .*

According to a handwritten copy of this poem in the Barthou collection it was composed at Rethel in November 1878. The annotated copy is almost certainly wrong therefore in stating 'Mons 7bre 1874, même lieu'.

iv. *Mon Dieu m'a dit . . .*

There are four different dates to be considered for this celebrated sequence of ten sonnets. It was sent to Lepelletier in a letter dated 8 September 1874; in the manuscript of *Cellulairement* it was at first dated '20 août 1874'; this was crossed out and 'Mons, 15 janvier, sortie de prison' was substituted; finally the annotated copy gives 'Mons, septembre-octobre 1874'. The first date given in *Cellulairement* is undoubtedly the correct date of composition and is confirmed by the date of the letter to Lepelletier. The poem was in all probability inspired by Verlaine's taking communion on 15 August and thus completing the process of his return to full membership of the Christian faith.

The use of the traditional form of the sonnet in alexandrines—for the first time since *Poèmes saturniens*, with the exception of *L'espoir luit* . . . - (III iii) and perhaps one or two other poems—could be symbolic of this return to the church, but it is interesting to note the extent to which Verlaine nevertheless maintains a characteristic fluidity in, for example, the first eight lines of the first sonnet, with their extreme amount of *njambement*, and the whole of the fourth sonnet, where the lines are so broken up that the usual structure of both the alexandrine and the sonnet has been destroyed. It should be noted too how frequently the caesura is displaced and even, on occasions, abolished altogether, as in the ninth line of the seventh sonnet, the eighth, ninth and twelfth lines of the next to last sonnet, and the second line of the final sonnet (see also the note to I iii, p. 78).

The would-be explanatory footnote: 'St Augustin', appended by Verlaine to the eighth line of the fourth sonnet, is to be found in a more helpful, expanded form in the manuscript version of the poem sent to Lepelletier where it reads: ' "Dieu nous a aimés jusqu'à la folie" (St. Augustin)'.

Though the obvious source of these sonnets is the First Commandment, there could perhaps be an echo too of George Herbert's poem *Love bade me welcome*:

> Love bade me welcome; yet my soul drew back
>> Guilty of dust and sin.
> But quick-ey'd Love, observing me grow slack
>> From my first entrance in,
> Drew nearer to me, sweetly questioning
>> If I lack'd anything.
>
> 'A guest', I answer'd, 'worthy to be here'.
>> Love said, 'You shall be he'.
> 'I, the unkind, the ungrateful? Ah, my dear,
>> I cannot look on Thee'.
> Love took my hand and smiling did reply,
>> 'Who made the eyes but I?'.
>
> 'Truth, Lord; but I have marr'd them: let my shame
>> Go where it doth deserve'.
> 'And know you not', says Love, 'who bore the blame?
>> 'My dear, then I will serve'.
> 'You must sit down', says Love, 'and taste my meat'.
>> So I did sit and eat.

In Verlaine's sonnet sequence certain lines seem particularly close to the ideas expressed in Herbert's poem, especially the following lines in the 2nd, 3rd and 7th sonnets:

... ô vous, toute lumière
Sauf aux yeux dont un lourd baiser tient la paupière.

—Il faut m'aimer! Je suis l'universel Baiser
Je suis cette paupière et je suis cette lèvre ...

Aime-moi! Ces deux mots sont mes verbes suprêmes,
Car étant ton Dieu tout-puissant, je peux vouloir,
Mais je ne veux d'abord que pouvoir que tu m'aimes.

Puis franchement et simplement viens à ma Table
Et je t'y bénirai d'un repas délectable ...

III

i. *Désormais le Sage* ...

'Arras, automne 1875' according to the annotated copy. The date is probably correct since the untroubled confidence Verlaine displays in his ability to play the part of 'le Sage', the man who can remain detached from the world, suggests a date fairly soon after his conversion—I iii has the same kind of theme in the last four stanzas. The last stanza of this poem no doubt explains why it opens the third section since there are a good many landscapes in the later part of this section.

ii. *Du fond du grabat* ...

There can be no doubt that the date given in the annotated copy 'Ecrit à Paris, hiver 1879' is wrong, since this poem, which is one of the few obscure and difficult poems that Verlaine wrote, figures in *Cellulairement* where it is dated: 'Mons, juin-juillet 1874'. The theme of the poem too suggests that it was composed shortly before Verlaine's communion on 15 August and the final lines in fact make it a kind of prelude to the sonnet sequence (II iv). In *Cellulairement*, echoing the Latin term for Christ's way to the cross, the poem bore the title 'Via dolorosa' and it describes the stages by which Verlaine was led towards his conversion. In the annotated copy there are brief comments in the margin opposite each stanza; 1st stanza: 'Impressions de Paris en décembre 1871'; 2nd and 3rd stanzas: 'Souvenir de Charleville, Xbre'; 4th stanza: 'Charleroi, 1872'; 5th stanza: 'Bruxelles 1872'; 6th stanza: 'Allusion à ma femme'; 7th stanza: 'Traversée d'Ostende à Douvres, 1872'; 8th and 9th stanzas: 'Londres, 1872'; 11th stanza: 'Bruxelles, juillet-août, 1873'; 12th and 13th stanzas: 'Mons, août 1874'; 14th and 15th stanzas: 'Mons, août—7bre, 1874'.
The 'grabat' in line 1 could well refer to the one in the room in the

Rue Campagne-Première where Rimbaud lived when he first came to Paris and where Verlaine joined him in January 1872 after quarrelling with his wife. The 'étoile' of line 2 is no doubt symbolic of the purity which Verlaine desired and the loss of which he regretted. The last few lines express the profound sense of disquiet which Verlaine felt at that time, as is evidenced by the sonnet *Vers pour être calomnié* (in *Jadis et Naguère* but originally intended for *Sagesse* and figuring in the manuscript presented to Mathilde where it is, however, crossed out) in which he anxiously asks Rimbaud: 'Vite, éveille-toi. Dis, l'âme est immortelle?'

In the second stanza the 'aigre trompette' of line 14, to which Verlaine added the adjective 'bavaroise' in the margin of the annotated copy, refers to the German occupation of Charleville, through which Verlaine passed on his way back to Paris from Paliseul where he spent Christmas 1871. The pronoun 'on' in the following lines could suggest that Rimbaud accompanied him in this journey through the Ardennes.

The snow covered landscape seen through the 'cadre étroit' of a train window is the theme of the 3rd stanza, lines 21–30, where the snow becomes a second symbol of the purity that Verlaine is seeking. Archangel is the English spelling of the town in Northern Russia which Verlaine, no doubt bearing in mind the literal meaning of the name, sees as the mysterious goal towards which he is striving, like a desert traveller in pursuit of a mirage.

The 4th stanza, lines 31–40, describes Charleroi, one of the two towns along with Walcourt, through which Verlaine and Rimbaud passed on their way to Brussels after the former had finally abandoned his wife and family on 7 July 1872. The *Paysages belges* section of *Romances sans Paroles* includes a poem on each of these two towns. There is again the anxious questioning note in the last two lines of this stanza.

The 5th stanza, lines 41–50, describes the life Rimbaud and Verlaine led in Brussels in July and August 1872 and the elder poet's desperate attempt to still the 'voix intime' within him as he crosses the threshold into Rimbaud's world and soars up into the paradise he has been promised. Again however the words 'crime' and 'sanglant' betray Verlaine's disquiet about Rimbaud's philosophy and the last two lines reveal a longing to turn away from this false ideal and to return to the security of childhood.

The 6th stanza, lines 51–60, according to the marginal note in the annotated copy, refers to Mathilde and in the third and fourth lines and the last two lines it seems that Verlaine may be quoting his own comments on his wife two years before when he believed that she had betrayed him—compare, for example, the lines in 'Birds in the Night' in *Romances sans Paroles*: 'vos yeux . . . ne couvaient plus rien que la trahison', and the opening paragraph of Verlaine's letter to Lepelletier on

4—S • •

8 November 1872 where he writes of Mathilde's 'immonde accusation', her 'inouïes perfidies' and her 'mensonges et ruses', for which he felt, according to his letter to Lepelletier two days later, 'un parfait mépris, quelque chose comme le sentiment des talons de bottes pour les crapauds' (*Correspondance*, i, pp. 55 and 64). In lines 55 and 56 Verlaine appears to be protesting that Mathilde had refused to understand and to forgive his relationship with Rimbaud and in lines 57 and 58 to be reproaching her for being so rash as to presume to pass judgement.

In the 7th stanza, lines 61–70, describing the Channel crossing, Verlaine visualises the sea, in a traditionally symbolic way, as a maternal figure consoling him in his sorrow.

The 8th stanza, lines 71–80, looks back at the months spent in London with Rimbaud in late 1872 from Verlaine's new vantage point so that he now recognises that he was, at that time, unaware of the direction his life was taking; his high hopes of a new kind of life with Rimbaud led in fact to despair and finally to his present state where he is not quite ready to dedicate himself to God.

The 9th stanza, lines 81–90, continues this theme of being on the verge of salvation, a salvation coming from someone whose influence Verlaine has for long rejected, until now when his dream of attaining an ideal world with Rimbaud has been shattered so that he needs someone to save him from the shipwreck of his hopes.

The 10th stanza, lines 91–100, also continues this theme of waiting for the moment of communion with God and adds to it the theme of divine guidance, freeing Verlaine from all care for the future and all reproaches for the past.

The opening line of the 11th stanza, lines 101–10, echoes the opening poem of *Sagesse* and offers the same paradox that unhappiness has brought happiness, as he now realises looking back at the events of July and August 1873 in Brussels. This paradox is continued in the rest of the stanza in the image of the thorn which has pierced his side and his heart, like the lance of the 'bon chevalier masqué' in I i, and yet which has healing powers.

The 'deux cœurs' in the 12th stanza, lines 111–20, could refer either to Rimbaud and Mathilde, or to Verlaine and Mathilde, or to Verlaine and Rimbaud, but the last seems the most likely solution since a reconciliation with Rimbaud would be quite incompatible with Verlaine's return to Christianity, so that this is an episode Verlaine must put behind him, even if with regret. The final somewhat obscure lines of this stanza appear to mean that just as an animal is unaware of the vital importance of its brain, so, by analogy, man can be unaware of the vital process of belief in God that is taking place within him.

The first two lines of stanza 13, lines 121–30, seem to repeat this theme and appear to mean that the body is unaware of the change that is taking place in the mind. The remaining lines of this stanza undoubtedly refer to Rimbaud, the 'tenace démon' who, in the passage *Vagabonds* of the *Illuminations* mentions a pact with Verlaine as the latter does here: 'J'avais en effet, en toute sincérité d'esprit, pris l'engagement de le rendre à son état primitif de fils du Soleil . . .' In this stanza there is therefore a momentary resurgence of the Verlaine of 1872 and early 1873 rejecting Christianity and the prospect of eternal bliss in favour of Rimbaud's more immediate goals.

In stanza 14 too, lines 131–40, there is a resurgence of an earlier Verlaine, but this time the Verlaine consumed with hatred for Mathilde, the 'vipère des bois' already referred to in stanza 6 who recurs here. Line 35: 'Cette fois tu mords', is presumably a reference to Mathilde, the 'vipère des bois' already referred to in stanza 6 who recurs shortly before, in April 1874. But the stanza ends with the new Verlaine striving to achieve a sense of detachment from the past.

Stanza 15, lines 141–50, continues this theme, as Verlaine appeals for gentleness, patience and tranquillity and, in lines 147 and 148, for a simple, naïve faith springing from the heart more than from reason.

The poem ends in lines 151–60 with a plea for the banishment of pride, the sin of Cain, in favour of humility such as Abel had, and in this state of humble repentance Verlaine has finished his 'via dolorosa' and is ready for communion with God.

It should be noted that the poem is in 'vers impairs' of five syllables grouped in ten line stanzas arranged as two quatrains and a rhyming couplet.

iii. *L'espoir luit . . .*

This is another of the few poems by Verlaine whose meaning is obscure and is disputed by the critics. In *Cellulairement* it was dated 'Bruxelles, octobre 1873' and it was sent to Lepelletier in a letter dating from the beginning of October 1873 as one of a group of four poems under the collective title: 'Mon almanach pour 1874', which was slightly modified in *Cellulairement* to read: 'Mon almanach pour l'année passée'. But in the annotated copy the poem is dated 'Jehonville, Belgique, été 1873' and its individual title is 'Eté' both in the letter to Lepelletier and in *Cellulairement*. It is for this reason that many critics, such as L. Morice in his critical edition of *Sagesse* and A. Fongaro in an article on the poem in the *Revue des sciences humaines*, 1955, pp. 227–56, have taken the reference to the 'brin de paille dans l'étable' in a literal rather than a symbolic sense and have assumed that the setting of the poem is a country inn. In point of fact however Verlaine was not in Jehonville in the summer of 1873. He was there from early April, after he and Rimbaud had left London and gone their separate ways, until late in May when they joined forces again and returned to London, but throughout the summer he was either in London or in Brussels. It seems therefore more likely that the 'brin de paille' should be taken in its usual metaphorical sense of the straw at which a drowning man clutches, particularly since the reference to a ray of hope suggests the same idea. It is conceivable that Verlaine could have had in mind the possibility of a reconciliation with his wife, as L. Morice and A. Fongaro believe, but it seems more probable that he was thinking of the outcome of his trial in Brussels and particularly of his appeal against his sentence, which was heard on 27 August 1873. It is instructive in this connection to note that in *Mes Prisons* Verlaine was to write: 'Et le jour de l'appel luisit, si j'ose m'exprimer ainsi. Luisit! Car quel beau temps ce jour-là, quel soleil!— Moi, du nord, j'admire, j'aime peu le soleil, il me cause des nausées, il m'étourdit, il m'aveugle . . .' (*Œuvres complètes*, ii, p. 763).

There are therefore good grounds for thinking that the poem depicts Verlaine sitting in his cell (for which 'étable' is substituted as a natural consequence of the use of the expression 'brin de paille') tormented both literally by a wasp and probably figuratively by worry, and concentrating on the literal and figurative ray of light penetrating the darkness of his cell and the blackness of his situation.

In view of the protective and even maternal tone of the second quatrain it may be that it is not, as one might have expected, the prison warder, but Verlaine's mother who offers her son a refreshing drink of water—a standard feature of prison diet but not, it may be noted, the kind of thing that Verlaine, of all people, was likely to drink in a country inn.

If this explanation of the second quatrain is accepted—and it should be remembered that Verlaine's mother had rushed to Brussels on 5 July in response to a telegram from him, had been present at the shooting incident and remained with him until early September after the decision of the Court of Appeal—then the woman who, in the first tercet, enters Verlaine's dream, her footsteps being evoked by the strokes of the clock at noon half penetrating the sleeping prisoner's mind, must be Mathilde.

In the final tercet the repeat of 'midi sonne' can be explained by the fact that Verlaine wakes up and realises that it is indeed the twelve strokes of noon that he has heard. He then falls alseep again, consoled by his mother's words, although the last, strangely detached and poignant line may well come from Verlaine himself, already fearing that the decision of the Court of Appeal will go against him and that the month of September, due to begin in a few days time, will be one which he will not be able to enjoy for another two years.

iv. *Gaspard Hauser chante*:

'Bruxelles (prison des Petits-Carmes, août 1873, après ma condamnation)', according to both *Cellulairement* and the annotated copy.

Gaspard Hauser was reputed to be the son of Stéphanie de Beauharnais, niece of the Empress Joséphine and wife of the Grand Duke Charles of Baden. He was said to have been stolen from his cradle soon after his birth in 1812 and from then on led a vagabond existence until he was assassinated in 1833. Verlaine evidently felt a kind of affinity with the strange, wandering life of Gaspard Hauser who also figures in a long passage entitled *Scenario pour ballet* in *Les mémoires d'un veuf*.

v. *Un grand sommeil noir* . . .

'Br. le 8 août 1873' according to *Cellulairement*, confirmed by the annotated copy which states, referring to the preceding poem: 'Même lieu et même date'. The 8 August 1873 was the day of Verlaine's trial and these three quatrains were obviously written immediately after sentence was pronounced. It is interesting and significant to note the similarities of theme and vocabulary between this poem and 'L'espoir luit . . .', in both of which Verlaine dwells on the ideas of sleep and childhood and uses such terms as 'dormir', 'espoir', 'berceau' or 'bercé' and 'creux'. This is another reason for thinking that 'L'espoir luit . . .' is concerned with the same kind of circumstances as 'Un grand sommeil noir . . .' and was written at about the same time.

The second stanza is a clear reference to the ideas advanced by Rimbaud and contains an echo of the latter's phrase in the passage 'Matinée d'ivresse' of the *Illuminations*: 'On nous a promis d'enterrer dans l'ombre l'arbre du bien et du mal'. Verlaine himself had already referred to these ideas of Rimbaud's in 'Crimen amoris', written in July 1873 and intended for *Cellulairement* but finally included, in a slightly different form, in *Jadis et Naguère*. In the course of the poem Verlaine puts the following words in the mouth of 'le plus beau d'entre tous ces mauvais anges', who is, of course, Rimbaud:

Vous le saviez, qu'il n'est point de différence

Entre ce que vous dénommez Bien et Mal.

Qu'au fond des deux vous n'avez que la souffrance.

Je veux briser ce Pacte trop anormal.

The third stanza introduces the same desire for protection and comfort that can be perceived in 'L'espoir luit . . .' and again the explanation may well be that Mme. Verlaine, on hearing the sentence, rushed down to Verlaine's cell to console her son in his grief.

vi. *Le ciel est, par-dessus le toit* . . .

'Bruxelles, Petits Carmes, à la pistole, septembre 1873', according to the annotated copy and the evident distress this poem reveals confirms that this date is broadly correct, although when quoting the poem in *Mes Prisons* (*Œuvres complètes*, ii, pp. 757–9) Verlaine implies that it was written somewhat earlier, before his trial on 8 August. One of the paragraphs from this passage in *Mes Prisons* is worth quoting since it describes the scene which inspired the poem: 'Par-dessus le mur de devant ma fenêtre (j'avais une fenêtre, une vraie! munie, par example, de longs et rapprochés barreaux), au fond de la si triste cour où s'ébattait, si j'ose ainsi parler, mon mortel ennui, je voyais, c'était en août, se balancer la cime aux feuilles voluptueusement frémissantes de quelque haut peuplier d'un square ou d'un boulevard voisin. En même temps m'arrivaient des rumeurs lointaines, adoucies, de fête (Bruxelles est la ville la plus bonhommement rieuse et rigoleuse que je sache). Et je fis, à ce propos, ces vers qui se trouvent dans *Sagesse* . . .' (*Œuvres complètes*, ii, p. 758).

The use of repetition in these lines should be noted as adding much to the simplicity and musicality of the poem.

vii. *Je ne sais pourquoi* . . .

The date given in *Cellulairement*, 'Bruxelles, juillet 1873', seems preferable to the one given in the annotated copy, 'Bruxelles, septembre 1873' since the poem, however obscure it may be on many points, leaves little room for doubt that it was written before Verlaine's condemnation and even before his arrest. In view of its sea setting, and bearing in mind that in *Cellulairement* it was entitled *Sur les eaux*, it seems in fact extremely probable that it was initially inspired as early as 3 July 1873, the day on which Verlaine crossed the Channel alone after a violent quarrel with Rimbaud in London.

This gives a virtually literal sense to the first three lines but the next three remain somewhat ambiguous in that they could refer to Verlaine's feelings either towards Mathilde, or towards Rimbaud, or towards both, although a precise identification of what it is that Verlaine is seeking (in *Cellulairement* he wrote 'cherche' instead of 'couve') is not of course indispensible to appreciating the poem.

The second stanza continues the analogy Verlaine implied in the first stanza between himself and a bird and in these five lines he appears to be recognising his own instability and vacillation. Although the image is different, one is reminded of the last stanza of 'Chanson d'automne' in

Poèmes saturniens:

> 'Et je m'en vais
> Au vent mauvais
> Qui m'emporte
> Deçà, delà,
> Pareil à la
> Feuille morte.

The third stanza, like the first, has a certain ambiguity about it. The word 'liberté' has led some critics to suppose that the poem was written in prison when Verlaine was first arrested, but if it was in fact written on 3 July Verlaine could be expressing a desire to be freed from Rimbaud's influence. The first line however, 'ivre de soleil' has a 'Rimbaldian' ring and is reminiscent of the opening of the final paragraph of 'Vagabonds' in the *Illuminations*: 'J'avais en effet, en toute sincérité d'esprit, pris l'engagement de le rendre à son état primitif de fils du Soleil . . .' Even though he had just left Rimbaud, Verlaine had done so in a fit of temper and was no doubt still influenced by his ideas.

In the fourth stanza the element of self pity so often encountered in Verlaine appears, as he describes, still maintaining the symbol of the sea bird, the pain and sorrow life inflicts on him.

The fifth stanza is a repeat of the first and the poem ends as it began on a note of bewilderment, reminiscent of the end of 'Il pleure dans mon cœur . . .' in *Romances sans Paroles*, as Verlaine wonders why he should feel afraid of seeking what is dear to him.

The extreme originality of the rhythms used in 'Je ne sais pourquoi . . .' is worthy of note. Not only is the poem in 'vers impairs' but these are of three different kinds, the first, third and fifth stanzas being made up of two lines of five syllables followed by a line of thirteen syllables with this pattern repeated in the last three lines of these six line stanzas. The second and fourth stanzas however are made up of five lines, each of nine syllables.

The rhyme scheme too is noteworthy in that the first, third and fourth stanzas are in exclusively masculine rhymes and the second and fourth in exclusively feminine rhymes. This emphasises the difference in tone between the two kinds of stanzas, the first, third and fifth having a positive quality to them as the seagull flies on its way, while the second and fourth have a negative quality as it is buffeted by the wind and waves.

viii. *Parfums, couleurs, systèmes, lois!* . . .

'Mons, fin 1874 (prison)', states the annotated copy, no doubt correctly since the strong religious fervour expressed in this poem clearly indicates that it was written shortly after Verlaine's conversion. Its general theme is the rejection of the world of man in favour of the world of God and it bears some relation to 'Petits amis qui sûtes nous prouver . . .' which also dismisses human wisdom in favour of divine revelation. 'Parfums, couleurs, systèmes, lois' and 'les mots' symbolise the whole range of human activities which are as nothing compared with the figure of Christ on the cross. The second tercet seems to suggest that Verlaine is having to struggle against temptation, to crush his dreams underfoot and to resist the 'voix tentatrice des foules'. The two quatrains are even more obscure but their meaning appears to be that Verlaine's gaze is directed towards heaven and that consequently the objects of this world—flowers (other than heavenly flowers—the pun on 'calice' meaning both 'chalice' and 'calyx' is impossible in English) wine, women and nights devoted to love—these delights are a torture for one of the damned who aspires to be one of the saints.

The form of the poem should be noted since it is an 'inverted sonnet', with the tercets preceding the quatrains, a form that Verlaine uses on several occasions and that cannot usually be considered to have any sexual significance except perhaps in the case of 'Le Bon Disciple', the manuscript of which was discovered by the Brussels police in Rimbaud's wallet in July 1873, (see *Œuvres poétiques complètes*, pp. 215 and 1108).

ix. *Le son du cor . . .*

'Jehonville (Belgique), ressouvenir de Charleville, hiver 1872' according to the annotated copy. But Verlaine spent the winter of 1872 in London and did not go to Jehonville until April 1873. He had however passed through Charleville in December 1871 and the second and third stanzas of 'Du fond du grabat' are also a 'ressouvenir de Charleville'. There is in fact some similarity between the two poems; in the one there is an 'aigre trompette' and in the other 'le son du cor s'afflige'; in the one the trumpet call is made from 'au bas du rempart' and in the other it dies away 'au bas de la colline'; the 'vent du coteau' in the one is echoed by 'la bise' in the other; and both are concerned with a snow covered landscape. It seems therefore probable that this poem, which could well have been included in *Romances sans Paroles* rather than *Sagesse*, is a recollection of Charleville in the winter of 1871 even if it was not actually written until the spring of 1873. There is an obvious echo in the first line of Vigny's line: 'Le son du cor est triste au fond du bois' and a perhaps less obvious echo of a line from Baudelaire's 'Harmonie du soir': 'Le violon frémit comme un cœur qu'on afflige'.

x. *La tristesse, la langueur du corps humain . . .*

'Arras, été 1875', according to the annotated copy, but there is some ressemblance between this poem and the sonnet 'Vers pour être calomnié':

Ce soir je m'étais penché sur ton sommeil.
Tout ton corps dormait chaste sur l'humble lit,
Et j'ai vu, comme un qui s'applique et qui lit,
Ah! j'ai vu que tout est vain sous le soleil! . . .

Ah! misère de t'aimer, mon frêle amour
Qui vas respirant comme on expire un jour!
O regard fermé que la mort fera tel! . . .

Vite, éveille-toi. Dis, l'âme est immortelle?

Though finally published in *Jadis et Naguère* this poem, as mentioned
above (see notes to III ii), was at first intended to form part of *Sagesse*
There is no doubt that it is about Rimbaud and it was probably
written in 1873 when Verlaine was becoming increasingly disquieted
by Rimbaud's ideas. 'La tristesse, la langueur du corps humain' could
also therefore be about Rimbaud and may have been written at
approximately the same time. This possibility is given added weight by
the fact that both sonnets are in 'vers impairs' of eleven syllables and
that both create an impression of false rhymes in the quatrains by using
the same rhymes in masculine and feminine forms—in 'La tristesse,
la langueur du corps humain' 'apitoient' and 'foudroient', the only
two feminine rhymes in the poem, are echoed by 'décroît' and 'toit'
and in 'Vers pour être calomnié' 'sommeil' and 'soleil' are echoed
by 'merveille' and 'm'éveille', and 'l'humble lit' and 'qui lit' by 'plie'
and 'folie', while there is an actual false rhyme in the tercets between
'tel' and 'immortelle'.

The curious and obscure fourth line: 'Quand les draps zèbrent la
peau, foulent la main', could perhaps be an allusion to a bandaged hand
and the whole poem may therefore refer specifically to Rimbaud lying ill
after being shot in the wrist by Verlaine on 10 July 1873. This could
also explain the 'fièvre du demain' and the 'bain de sueur qui décroît',
as well as the various words and expressions suggesting weakness—
'mièvre', 'comme un oiseau qui grelotte', 'la chair frémissante, frêle
décor', 'triste corps, combien faible et combien puni'. The admirable
twelfth and thirteenth lines seems a particularly apt comment on
Rimbaud's vain search for an ideal world:

Et les yeux, les pauvres yeux si beaux où point
La douleur de voir encore du fini!

But whether or not the poem was inspired by these circumstances, it
also has a wider significance and can be read simply as a moving
comment on the frailty of the flesh.

xi. *La bise se rue à travers . . .*

This poem, like 'L'espoir luit . . .' (III iii), formed part of the group of four poems sent to Lepelletier at the beginning of October 1873 and later included in *Cellulairement* (see the note to III iii on p. 91). In *Cellulairement* it shares with its three companion poems the date: 'Bruxelles, octobre 1873', but in the annotated copy it is dated: 'Jehonville, mai 1873, à travers champs'. This apparent contradiction can be largely resolved by the fact that in the letter to Lepelletier and in *Cellulairement* the poem consisted only of fourteen lines which were no doubt written during the weeks Verlaine spent in Jehonville after leaving London early in April 1873 and before returning there late in May of that year accompanied by Rimbaud. The last six lines however were added in prison, though it seems probable, judging by their theme, that they were composed, not as early as October 1873, as *Cellulairement* states, but in the spring of 1874 when Verlaine's thoughts were turning towards God. They appear for the first time in the second manuscript of *Sagesse* which also alters line 14 from its original reading: ' "Voici l'Avril!" Vieux cœur, allons!'. The two words in quotation marks may be taken from Browning's celebrated line: 'O to be in England, now that April's here', in which case the first part of the poem may date from 24 May 1873 when Verlaine and Rimbaud set off together for London for the last time. V. P. Underwood suggests (op. cit., p. 229) that the additional lines may date from as late as 1875 and that the second version of line 14: 'Debout mon âme, vite, allons', may be an echo of the opening lines of the well-known hymn that Verlaine had no doubt heard at Stickney: 'Awake, my soul, and with the sun Thy daily stage of duty run . . .'

xii. *Vous voilà, vous voilà, pauvres bonnes pensées . . .*

'Arras, été 1875' according to the annotated copy, and this humble resolve to lead a better life is typical of Verlaine at this period—compare I vi, 'O vous comme un qui boite au loin . . .' The quotation from Dante's *Il Purgatorio* which, as mentioned in the notes to I ii, Verlaine was reading in the summer of 1875, comes from Canto III, lines 79–84.

xiii. *L'échelonnement des haies . . .*

'Stickney, on a Sunday, 1875' according to the annotated copy; 'Stick. 1875' according to the first manuscript of *Sagesse*; and 'Stickney 1875' according to the second edition of *Sagesse*. The poem was however sent to Lepelletier in a letter dated 2 August 1877 and another manuscript copy exists with the date, 'July 1877'. There seems nevertheless little doubt that the earlier date is the correct one, particularly in view of the fact that the two later copies are entitled 'Paysage en Lincolnshire' and 'Paysage de Lincolnshire' and it was only from the spring of 1875 to the spring of 1876 that Verlaine was in that part of England.

The analogy between land and sea is an obvious one to use in the Fenlands, where the hedges do indeed look like waves running across the completely flat countryside. The poem is neatly rounded off by a return to a sea metaphor in the last stanza, but this time in reference to the sound of church bells. The 'impair' rhythm of seven syllable lines should be noted. In lines 10 and 11 the rhyme is permissible because the same word, 'aussi', has different meanings, in the first case 'also' and in the second case 'as'.

xvi. *L'immensité de l'humanité . . .*

'Londres, 1875', as in the annotated copy, is no doubt correct, the date given in the second edition of *Sagesse*, 'Londres, 75–7', being merely an indication of the period of time Verlaine spent in England, though not strictly in London, after his imprisonment. He was clearly impressed by the size, the historic importance, and the prosperity of the capital, as well as by its celebrated fog which he refers to in lines 7 and 8. The last two lines reveal Verlaine's almost militant catholicism in his conviction that Anglican London is ripe for conversion to the Roman faith.

xv. *La mer est plus belle . . .*

Originally entitled 'La mer de Bournemouth' this poem is dated 'Bournemouth 1877' in the first manuscript of *Sagesse*, 'Juin 1877' in another manuscript copy, 'Bournemouth 1877' in the second edition of *Sagesse* and it was sent to Lepelletier in a letter dated 2 August 1877. So the summer of 1877 seems a more convincing date than the preceding summer as stated in the annotated copy: 'Bournemouth, Angleterre, été 1876', especially as Verlaine in fact arrived there only in September of that year.

The last two lines of the first stanza are taken from the original version of the seventh stanza of 'Du fond du grabat' where the sea is also seen as a mother figure. It has been suggested by V. P. Underwood (*Verlaine et l'Angleterre*, pp. 306–7) that Verlaine was influenced by a passage from Tennyson's *Sea Dreams* comparing cliffs to cathedral fronts and that the first two lines reply to this analogy by contending that the sea is more beautiful than the cathedral fronts of the cliffs. Tennyson goes on to describe 'The Virgin Mother standing with her child High up on one of those dark minster fronts' and it may be that Verlaine too, in lines 5 and 6 visualises the Virgin Mary physically dominating the sea. But it may alternatively be that he sees her simply as watching over those at sea in an abstract way as he had done towards the end of 'Birds in the Night' in *Romances sans Paroles*. The 'impair' rhythm in lines of five syllables should be noted, and the unusual rhyme scheme with exclusively masculine and exclusively feminine rhymes in alternate stanzas.

xvi. *La 'grande ville'! . . .*

'Paris 1877' according to both the first manuscript and the second edition of *Sagesse*, a date which seems more probable than the one given in the annotated copy: 'Mars 1876', since Verlaine was then at Stickney. The theme of the poem is very like that of 'Désormais le Sage . . .' (III i), with the same mistrust of city life and the same preference for a 'Thébaïde', a place of solitude, far from the madding crowd. In the annotated copy Verlaine added an explanatory note about the last line indicating that the 'deux parts de mon âme' referred to his wife and son, though strictly speaking the reference is to his feelings for them.

xvii. *Tournez, tournez, bons chevaux de bois . . .*

This poem, in 'vers impairs' of nine syllables, was written in August 1872, some months before any other poem in *Sagesse*, after a visit to a Brussels fairground when Verlaine was wandering across Belgium with Rimbaud. It was published in *Romances sans Paroles* and it is difficult to understand why Verlaine should also have included it in *Sagesse*. It is true that there are some minor differences between the two poems—in the second stanza 'l'enfant tout rouge et la mère blanche' sedately replace 'le gros soldat, la plus grosse bonne', stanzas five and six are absent from the *Romances sans Paroles* version, the eighth stanza, like the second, has become rather more respectable than the original version which reads:

> Et dépêchez, chevaux de leur âme:
> Déjà voici que la nuit qui tombe
> Va réunir pigeon et colombe
> Loin de la foire et loin de madame,

and the original third line of the last stanza: 'Voici partir l'amante et l'amante' has also changed its character in the *Sagesse* version.

But even so Verlaine must have realised that the two poems were far too much alike and he withdrew 'Tournez, tournez, bons chevaux de bois' from the second edition of *Sagesse* in 1889, substituting for it the two following poems:

> Toutes les amours de la terre
> Laissent au cœur du délétère
> Et de l'affreusement amer,

Fraternelles et conjugales,
Paternelles et filiales,
Civiques et nationales,
Les charnelles, les idéales,
Toutes ont la guêpe et le ver.

La mort prend ton père et ta mère,
Ton frère trahira son frère,
Ta femme flaire un autre époux,
Ton enfant, on te l'aliène,
Ton peuple, il se pille ou s'enchaîne
Et l'étranger y pond sa haine,
Ta chair s'irrite et tourne obscène,
Ton âme flue en rêves fous.

Mais, dit Jésus, aime, n'importe!
Puis de toute illusion morte
Fais un cortège, forme un chœur,
Va devant, tel aux champs le pâtre,
Tel le coryphée au théâtre,
Tel le vrai prêtre ou l'idolâtre,
Tel les grands-parent près de l'âtre,
Oui, que devant aille ton cœur!

Et que toutes ces voix dolentes
S'élèvent rapides ou lentes,
Aigres ou douces, composant
A la gloire de Ma souffrance
Instrument de ta délivrance,
Condiment de ton espérance
Et mets de ta propre navrance,
L'hymne qui te sied à présent!

* * *

Sainte Thérèse veut que la Pauvreté soit
La reine d'ici-bas, et littéralement!
Elle dit peu de mots de ce gouvernement
Et ne s'arrête point aux détails de surcroît;

Mais le Point, à son sens, celui qu'il faut qu'on voie,
Et croie, est ceci dont elle la complimente:
Le libre arbitre pése, arguë et parlemente,
Puis le pauvre-de-cœur décide et suit sa voie.

Qui l'en empêchera? De vœux il n'en a plus
Que celui d'être un jour au nombre des élus,
Tout-puissant serviteur, tout-puissant souverain,

Prodigue et dédaigneux, sur tous, des choses eues,
Mais accumulateur des seules choses sues,
De quel si fier sujet, et libre, quelle reine!

The first of these two poems was written in 'Paris, 1884' according to the annotated copy (both the *Œuvres poétiques complètes* and the *Œuvres complètes* give this date incorrectly). By then Verlaine's period of 'sagesse' was long since over; Lucien Létinois had died the previous year and Verlaine had bought a farm at Coulommes where he spent most of his time drowning his sorrows in drink. His sense of failure and feeling of despair can be detected in the first two stanzas, although not all the details are autobiographical in that Verlaine's mother did not die until 1886 and his wife did not remarry until later the same year—unless, of course, the date given in the annotated copy is incorrect. In the last two stanzas there is an attempt to find consolation and hope in suffering that is perhaps reminiscent of Baudelaire's 'Bénédiction':

Soyez béni, mon Dieu qui donnez la souffrance
Comme un divin remède à nos impuretés.

The second poem is dated: 'Asile de Vincennes, juin 1887', according to the annotated copy (again the *Œuvres poétiques complètes* and the *Œuvres complètes* give this date incorrectly). Here too an autobiographical note can be detected in that at that date Verlaine was reduced to a state of utter destitution, and in this sonnet he is endeavouring to put a brave face on his situation. Saint Theresa of Avila emphasised the Christian virtue of poverty without, as Verlaine points out in lines 3 and 4, devoting too much space to this subject. The somewhat tortuous second stanza makes the point that having freely weighed, debated and discussed a problem it is the man who has no material possessions and no links with this world who is able to arrive at a decision. The tercets develop still further this point that it is the poor man who is disdainful of the things of this world and whose gaze is fixed on the next world. The extraordinary syntax of the final line makes it difficult to understand but it presumably refers back to the opening lines of the poem and to the idea of 'la pauvreté' as 'la reine d'ici-bas', and also the idea of the pride and independence of the man unhindered by material possessions, so that, if a normal syntax is re-established, the line means: 'quelle reine de quel sujet, fier et libre'. The rhyme scheme is unusual in that the second quatrain uses the same rhymes as the first quatrain but in feminine form, and the same is true of the two tercets, so that there is an impression of false rhymes.

xviii.   *Parisien, mon frère à jamais étonné . . .*

'Arras, 77' according to the first manuscript and the second edition of *Sagesse*, though this was altered to 'Arras, 1880', on the annotated copy.

The earlier date is probably the correct one, but more important than the date is the place of composition since this long poem is a detailed and admiring description of Arras, a town Verlaine knew very well since it was his mother's home town and he had often stayed there, or in the nearby village of Fampoux—the 'chez nous' referred to in line 14. In contrast with this are his disparaging asides about certain districts of Paris such as Montmartre and Pantin, whilst line 32: 'Au lieu du long ennui de vos haussmanneries' is an allusion to Baron Haussmann who virtually replanned and rebuilt Paris under the Second Empire.

xix. *C'est la fête du blé* . . .

'Fampoux, 77', according to the first manuscript and the second edition of *Sagesse*, although again this was altered in the annotated copy to: 'Fampoux, près d'Arras, juillet 1880'. The month certainly seems unlikely since this poem was clearly written at harvest time and by September 1880 *Sagesse* was completed. September 1877 seems therefore the more probable date, in between Verlaine's leaving Bournemouth and taking up his post at Rethel. 'Ces choses' in line 2 is a discreetly veiled allusion to the events in Verlaine's life from 1872–4. The poem is more complex than is usual with Verlaine in that the wheat harvest described in the first two stanzas calls to mind, in the last two lines of the third stanza, the grape harvest taking place further south. These two themes occur together in the fourth stanza and in the final stanza bread and wine are given a religious significance so as to bring *Sagesse* to a close on a religious note. V. P. Underwood (*Verlaine et l'Angleterre*, p. 230) sees in this poem echoes of a number of English hymns that celebrate harvest time. But as the grape harvest naturally plays no part in English hymns and as the 'sweet refreshing rain' that understandably figures in them so frequently is absent from Verlaine's poem, any influence there may be is no doubt of a very general nature.